The Reach and Grasp of Policy Analysis

Institute for Social Science Research
Monograph Series

General Editor, Philip B. Coulter

Political Voice: Citizen Demand for Urban Public Services, by Philip B. Coulter

Child Abuse in the Deep South: Geographical Modifiers of Abuse Characteristics, by Lee W. Badger, Nicholas A. Green, L. Ralph Jones, and Julia A. Hartman

The Reach and Grasp of Policy Analysis: Comparative Views of the Craft, by Richard I. Hofferbert

The Reach and Grasp of Policy Analysis

Comparative Views of the Craft

Richard I. Hofferbert

Published for the

Institute for Social Science Research by

The University of Alabama Press *Tuscaloosa and London*

Library of Congress Cataloging-in-Publication Data

Hofferbert, Richard I., 1937–
    The reach and grasp of policy analysis : comparative views of the
craft / Richard I. Hofferbert.
        p.   cm.—(Institute for Social Science Research monograph
series ; 3)
    Bibliography: p.
    Includes index.
    ISBN 0-8173-0464-9 (alk. paper)
    1. Policy sciences. I. University of Alabama. Institute for
Social Science Research. II. Title. III. Series.
H97.H58 1990
320′.6—dc20
                                                            89–4899
                                                            CIP

British Library Cataloguing-in-Publication Data available

For Mark

Contents

Tables

Figures

Preface

The art of policy analysis has many roots. Scholars, politicians, and many citizens have perennially been curious about why governments do what they do to and for people and about what effects these efforts have. But as in so many areas, it was in the United States that the *art* was transformed into a widespread *craft,* if not an industry of mass production. Research budgets, number of involved persons, and pages of print indicate that as a professional undertaking of social scientists, the craft, especially in its more modern "scientific" incarnation, has been most vigorously pursued in the United States.

The American preeminence, however, is waning for two reasons. First, research resources for policy analysis in the United States since the peak years of the 1970s, seem to have declined somewhat. More important, research endeavors elsewhere have increased significantly.

Policy analysis is becoming institutionalized in many countries. For example, in 1982, the program of the twelfth World Congress of the International Political Science Association (IPSA), in Rio de Janeiro, had, by the most generous count, about half a dozen panels (out of hundreds) devoted to empirical policy analysis. Three years later, at the Thirteenth World Congress, in Paris, more than a quarter of the program was clearly labeled "policy analysis," with national representation roughly equivalent to the membership of IPSA. Symmetry is emerging in the flow of policy analytic experience across countries.

The essays in this book are an effort at stock-taking, a view principally from the vantage of American experience, and that of it which is fit for export, as seen by a student of comparative politics.

The stimulus for such stock-taking has been a series of trips and visiting professorships in policy analysis at five institutions in three countries over nine years. In summer 1977, I was a visiting researcher at the Zentrum fur Umfragen, Methoden, und Analyse (ZUMA) in Mannheim, Germany. That was followed, during the fall semester, with a visiting appointment to teach policy analysis at the University of Mannheim. During 1981–82, under a program sponsored by the Organization for Economic Cooperation and Development (OECD), I was appointed to the social science faculty of Boğaziçi University in Istanbul, Turkey, to help inaugurate a graduate program in public policy and public management. For a brief few weeks in 1983, I had the magnificent opportunity to obtain a close-up view of a very poor country, walking through the remote hill villages of Nepal with my son Mark, who was a Peace Corps volunteer installing domestic water systems.

In the fall of 1985, I had the pleasure to be a visiting professor of policy analysis in Lausanne, Switzerland, at the Institute for Advanced Studies in Public Administration (Institut de Hautes Etudes en Administration Publique—IDHEAP), where I was encouraged to pull together my reflections on the state of the craft of policy analysis. This new institution, founded in 1981, has built a superb program of research and teaching. It has brought together a small group of generous, talented, and hospitable professionals, dedicated to high-quality teaching and research in the policy process. The schedule of lectures arranged for me by Raimund Germann, the able director of IDHEAP, was the specific impetus that pushed me to prepare much of the material in this volume. It was the best form of visiting professorship.

Finally, I served as visiting research professor in policy analysis at the Free University of Berlin during the winter semester of 1986, a noble setting in which to contemplate the art of governance and the craft of policy analysis.

I cannot pretend to have lived and felt as those whom I have visited. Yet I have learned two things from my experiences with academic tourism. First, one should never judge a country or a culture by those who leave it. Tourists, soldiers, business people, and visiting scholars are invariably a poor sample of their home populations. Second, the greatest gain from seeing other cultures is the insight it provides into one's own.

The essays in this volume could not have been written entirely at home. Yet they speak to the American experience with policy analysis. I hope they say something about what students of politics, in many different cultural contexts, can do to improve our understanding of the causes and consequences of the actions of governments.

My principal debts are to those who have been so gracious as to invite me into their workplaces and friendship circles: Max Kaase and Rudolf Wildenmann of ZUMA and the University of Mannheim; Ravi Kapil of OECD; Üstün Ergüder and my other friends and colleagues of Boğaziçi University; Raimund Germann of IDHEAP (Lausanne); and Hans-Dieter Klingemann, formerly of Zuma and now professor at the Free University of Berlin.

I am continuously grateful to my department (and its chair, Arthur S. Banks) at the State University of New York at Binghamton for the extraordinary patience and flexibility that have enabled me to keep my head up at home between frequent trips abroad.

Philip Coulter, director of the University of Alabama's Institute for Social Science Research and editor of the Social Science Monograph series, encouraged me to bring the book to publishable form. My colleague and friend Thomas Pasquarello offered very helpful criticism and the requisite amount of praise to keep me motivated. The manuscript was significantly improved by David Nachmias's able comments on an early draft and by Trudie Calvert's admirable editorial talent. They each and all have my sincere thanks.

The person who has had the most impact on my thinking about cross-national comparisons and particularly about public policies for very poor people is my son Mark Richard Hofferbert. He has packed more experience into his young years and has gained more capacity for hard-nosed moral assessment than many who have spent lifetimes combing the volumes of the world's best libraries.

Someday maybe I will write another book for another audience, which will, inadequately no doubt, relate the benefits I have gàined from traveling with Rose, a lady of stamina, sardonic wit, keen insight, and clarity of vision, who is, I am sure, the sole reason we ever get invited back anywhere.

Richard I. Hofferbert

The Reach and Grasp of Policy Analysis

PART I
Lessons from U.S. Experience?

The three chapters in Part 1 address the health and welfare of policy analysis in the United States, with emphasis on lessons provided by the American experience.

Chapter 1 reviews the rise and apparent decline of policy evaluation in the United States from the early 1960s through the 1980s. In that historical context, I try to show how the form and focus of policy evaluation were shaped by the spirit of optimism that fueled the American national policy process from the end of World War II until the later years of the Great Society. Likewise, the impact of alter gloominess is fitted to the apparent disillusionment that seeped into policy research. Special attention is given to the choice of models used by most policy analysts. The main point is to distinguish "product" research (for which I occasionally adopt the German label *Wirkungsforschung* from "process" research (to which I sometimes apply the Teutonic sobriquet *Vollzugsforschung*). *Vollzugsforschung,* I argue, has far greater long-term usefulness and political fit.

The "mapping" in Chapter 2 is aimed at dispelling undue pessimism about the health of U.S. policy analysis by suggesting that it is not so much disappearing as being institutionalized in numerous contexts which are rarely visible in well-known journals read by academic social scientists. The essay also argues for a mode of academic-government cooperation which implements the *Vollzugsforschung* or process model introduced in Chapter 1.

The discussion of applications to services for the elderly, in Chapter 3, reviews a few examples that illustrate the form and nature of research that is designed and executed cooperatively between academic researchers and public agencies. The history of the three projects of the Center for Social Analysis at the State University of New York at Binghamton demonstrates both the advantages and pitfalls of that relationship.

3

1

The Rise and Decline of the U.S. Policy Evaluation Industry

Lessons for Export?

Between 1960 and 1975, national research priorities drew many American social scientists out of the ivory tower and into the political arena, not as politicians or bureaucrats but as experts in the evaluation of public programs. Unprecedented quantities of government funds were provided to develop and sustain the new scholarly "industry" of policy evaluation.

By 1979, however, the boom appeared to be over, and social science research and development, especially as practiced under the label "policy evaluation," began an erratic decline, which appears to have lasted through the 1980s.

The trend lines in Figure 1.1 dramatically reveal the pattern. Social science research and development spending by the federal government rose from 1970 to 1978 at a rate comparable to the overall federal investment in research. After the late years of the Carter administration, however, unlike the general trend in research support, investment in social science sagged. A specific breakdown of figures is not necessary here, but a substantial share of the rise and decline in federal social science research and development funding involved contracted policy evaluation, and particularly evaluation of social service programs by extragovernment organizations, including both university institutes and nonacademic "think tanks."

Policy evaluation is the effort to employ social scientific research tools to *measure to what extent, under what conditions, and at what cost public programs attain their objectives.*[1] At its most sophisticated, it includes a wide range of research tools such as operations research, benefit-cost analysis, survey research, social-psychological measurement, computerized data management and analysis, and simulation. The specifics are not relevant to the concern here.

4

Figure 1.1   U.S. Federal Research Expenditures, 1970–1986

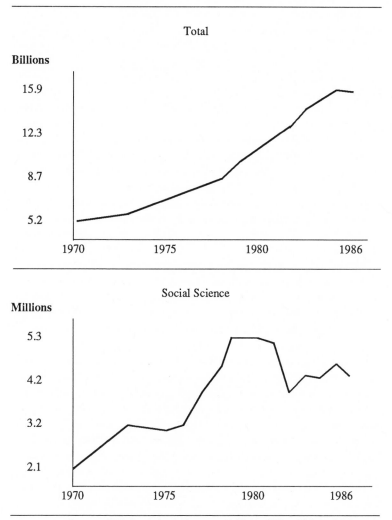

Source: *U.S. Statistical Abstract,* 1980 (p. 625), 1987 (p. 566).

Rather, my focus is on the rise and apparent decline of the American policy evaluation industry to see if there are any lessons that might be exportable to other settings where social science engagement in policy analysis is still on an upward trend.

The thesis is as follows: The American experience with policy evaluation was shaped and focused by the particular context of optimism in the American government through the 1960s. The structure and focus taken by social scientists can be said, in retrospect, to have minimized their long-term relevance and to have maximized their political vulnerability. The "industry" had a faulty model, and it produced an unpleasant message. The research apparatus was excessively centralized and never developed a stable clientele within public management. It could test outcomes of programs but could say little about improved delivery. What it did say was seldom heard. When the message was heard, it was often unpleasant. And the receivers shot the messenger. I shall argue, however, that the shooting was not fatal. The messenger has survived and is recovering, wiser for the wounds.

To see what led up to the shooting, I shall first discuss the context within which the American policy analysis industry arose, the Green Years.

The Green Years: Roots of Optimism

At the time John Kennedy moved into the White House, U.S. policy makers shared the general optimism that had grown up in the postwar years. That optimism was founded in both international and domestic success. We had helped win the war against fascism. Through the Marshall Plan we had helped finance and inspire the European economic miracle. We were the home base of the United Nations. Domestically, we seemed to have conquered the worst ravages of the business cycle. No depression had followed the war. We had taken the first definitive steps toward an apparent solution to our peculiar problem of racial discrimination.

Upon his inauguration, President Kennedy articulated the most optimistic definition of national purpose in the lifetimes of his constituents. We would put a man on the moon; and we did. We would stimulate our economic energies; and we did. With courage and determination, we would collectively accept responsibility for the condition of our least fortunate at home; and we tried.

Abroad, we would maintain with dignity and compassion our role as "leader of the free world." The Alliance for Progress would bring development to Latin America. No expression of our compassion and optimism was more dramatic than the Peace Corps. Through our partnerships in the North Atlantic Treaty Organization (NATO) and the UN, we would confront and convert the twin forces of poverty and totalitarianism.

John Kennedy could say "Allianza para el Progresso" and "Ich bin ein Berliner" almost without accent.

Some have called it *hubris,* others *naïveté.* But history was on our side; the list of accomplishments was positive and profound. Those were the Green Years.

The Gray Years were yet to come: Vietnam, Watergate, the weight of the bomb. Contrasted with Eisenhower's smile and Kennedy's rhetoric came the pictures of helicopters on top of the U.S. embassy in Saigon, Nixon's pathetic farewell, and Carter's grim visage after the failed rescue mission in the Iranian desert.

Well into the 1960s, the record of positive accomplishments was clear testimony not merely to the might of American private enterprise but to the newly discovered power of our public policy system. The war, the Marshall Plan, the Peace Corps, the space program, the steps toward racial equality, NATO, and the UN were not the products of a liberal market. They were monuments to public management.

Optimists saw these events as monuments to rational policy theory, to the capacity of political authorities to set goals and rationally to mobilize resources and monitor performance to assure the attainment of those goals. If we could build bombers for victory abroad and put an astronaut into orbit or a young Peace Corps volunteer into an African village, we could build a moral and just society at home.

We could apply the same fundamental tools of rational management, operations research, systems analysis, and their analogues to social engineering. The prewar enthusiasm for scientific management showed up in the 1960s as Planning, Programming, and Budgeting Systems, PPBS.

The basic assumption of scientific policy making was not that we knew answers to the big questions of social management but that we knew how to find answers. In the policy system, optimism was wide-spread that newly discovered tools of social science, some borrowed from economics but as many or more from business management and psychology, provided the means, if not for total foresight, at least for institutionalizing social learning.

As early as 1946 the Full Employment Act had set up the Council of Economic Advisors, supported by a system of economic data ac-quisition, monitoring, and management, to ensure steady progress against the perennially irregular patterns of economic fluctuation. By 1960, there were calls for a council of social advisers, to be supported likewise by a system of social indicators, for monitoring and managing social policy to iron out the moral irregularities and to keep us on a steady upward slope toward justice.

The Great Society: A Novel Theory of Policy Capacity

Kennedy's assassination was an overture to a movement in minor key—to the collective sobering that was to follow. His most immediate legacy, however, was an agenda of policy proposals, enhanced and implemented by the political genius of Lyndon Johnson. Johnson in-herited an agenda of policy proposals and a Zeitgeist, as well as the personnel who fashioned those policies and embodied that Geist.

They gave us Vietnam. But they also gave us the Great Society. The Great Society, with its War on Poverty, embodied a novel theory of the role of the central government in domestic life. The New Deal of Franklin Roosevelt had implemented known tools of the welfare state that had been tested on the European continent: workers' insurance, pensions for the elderly, income transfers for the poor. The New Deal moved money from the well-off to the less well-off fairly effectively.

The Great Society and other initiatives in its wake, however, were going to do more than move money. They would change personal values and the sociopolitical structure (Wildavsky, 1979). They would attack more than material conditions. They would get to the roots of what is often called the culture of poverty, especially acute in our biracial so-ciety.

Project Headstart, a preschool program for underprivileged children, and other educational projects for the disadvantaged, were to change the nature of individual motivation among American youth.

Community Action Programs were to change the very organizational and political life of poorer Americans, especially in the cities.

Training programs for teenagers (especially black teenagers) were to change not only their incomes but their orientations toward the world of work. A bewildering array of rehabilitation and anticrime programs was to change the nature of the criminal personality.

Programs for the aged were to ensure not only that old people had money but that they were independent and happy as well.

Drug and alcohol abuse were to be ameliorated through psychological counseling and various governmental-subsidized *support structures*.

Community-based mental health programs were to provide the means for deinstitutionalizing disturbed people and helping integrate them into rewarding, productive lives in the mainstream community.

The physical environment could be made pure, clean, and quiet without seriously threatening economic growth. Lady Bird Johnson planted tulips in Washington (for which I hope all visitors to that fair city are grateful).

Sex education, smuggled into the public school curriculum when not officially adopted, was expected to reduce teenage pregnancies, reduce the incidence of venereal disease, and, presumably, increase the number of happy nuclear families.

Bilingual education, nudged with federal dollars, was expected not only to facilitate the learning of English but also to ensure maintenance of ethnic pride and cultural awareness, especially among our Spanish-speaking young people.

The Great Society programs, and the legacy of them that remains, were to do more than move money. They were to change behavior and values. To quantity, as measured by income transfers, was added quality of life as an objective of public policy.

These aspirations also provided the key stimulus to a new mode of scholarly enterprise: the execution of grants and contracts of money for policy evaluation research.

A Sketch of the Industry

Systematic evaluation, using the entire arsenal of the behavioral sciences, fitted nicely into the optimism and faith in rationality of the 1960s.

From their relatively remote preserves on university campuses, social scientists were brought into the mainstream of government planning and administration. Many left the campus for the new "industry" of policy evaluation. In the Department of Health, Education, and Welfare (HEW), which was, early in the Nixon administration, to displace the Department of Defense as the largest consumer of federal money, was established the Office of Planning and Evaluation. One percent of the HEW budget was earmarked for evaluation.

Social science research was, for a time, the most rapidly growing area of spending by the National Science Foundation (NSF). Until it became politically unfashionable, money for social research from the Defense Department exceeded that from NSF. Unprecedented resources flowed from the federal government to the academy.

Many academic social scientists found it financially and administratively advantageous to set up shop off the campus. Research organizations such as the Rand Corporation, which had formerly concentrated on defense research, established policy evaluation branches. Rand established a doctoral program in policy analysis. New research centers such as Abt Associates in Cambridge, Massachusetts, headed by social scientists, grew over a few years from nothing to multi-million-dollar operations. Comparable rates of growth could be measured among the leading university-based social research centers such as the Institute for Social Research at the University of Michigan or the Institute for Research on Poverty at the University of Wisconsin–Madison.

Huge social experiments, using the best social scientific methods, were launched to test innovative programs such as the negative income tax for minimum income maintenance, housing allowances for rent support among the poor, and educational vouchers to maximize choice and innovation in elementary and secondary education. Hundreds of millions of dollars were expended on such experiments in the 1970s, all flowing through the policy evaluation industry.

The policy evaluation industry spawned a new breed of beneficiary of the federal budget, the so-called "Beltway Bandits," a series of consulting firms established along the superhighway that surrounds Washington, D.C., the Beltway.

By the most conservative estimate, over a quarter of a billion dollars was spent in 1973 by the federal government alone for social science research. A more realistic estimate would probably put the figure in excess of $500 million. Again by conservative estimate, by 1983, in constant dollars, that figure had declined by over 40 percent. At the same time there was an overall rate of increase of over 50 percent in total federal spending on research.

Many of the smaller think tanks have gone out of business. Most of the larger ones have cut back drastically on their personnel. University institutes have either diversified or declined.

A good argument can be made that the activity formerly contracted to the policy evaluation industry has been institutionalized under other organizational umbrellas, leaving the net quantity of actual policy evaluation as large as ever. Certainly the expanded policy role of the General Accounting Office, the Legislative Reference Service, and various intra-agency evaluation entities supports this thesis. The steady growth of state and local extension research by university policy research bureaus, which I discuss in Chapter 2, is another realm of institutionalization of evaluation (Haveman, 1987). It is interesting, however, that the private or academic policy evaluation industry should have shrunk at the very time when, in many realms of substantive policy, privatization has been on the rise.

Somewhere along the line, somebody was disappointed. The decline began during the Carter presidency so it was not caused by an anti-social-science bias of the Reagan administration. The disappointment was deeper and apparently nonpartisan.

A Faulty Model

The history of policy evaluation reveals two models. One views evaluation as a set of management tools: techniques for gathering information on the impact a program has during the process of service delivery; techniques for monitoring administrative performance and techniques for communicating that information and results of monitoring backward on a routine, institutionalized basis. This is research on implementation and feedback to policy administrators on the results of that research. The term *Volzugsforschung* is coming to be used in German and connotes a bit more of the intricacy of research engagement than does *implementation*. *Process* is the most reasonable approximation for *whole train research*, the literal translation.

This model, adapted from business administration and operations research, sees policy evaluation as embedded in the administrative process. As sketched in the right half of Figure 1.2, it envisions a series of incentives that enhance the receptivity of the program administrator to feedback on a program's impact on a short-term, routine basis. The *Vollzug* model is more than traditional management or administrative science, in that it focuses rigorously on social targets, that is, on real results and not merely on internal organizational processes. But it is still principally a management tool.[2]

Evaluation as a management tool is nonthreatening to the program administrator. It is a "servo" mechanism. It can be thought of as analogous to modern fuel injection systems in automobiles, whereby the mixture of inputs is adjusted to external temperature, humidity, and vehicle operation. The adjustment process is automatic and invisible to the external observer.

The other model of policy evaluation is less for management and more for measurement of long-term goal attainment, for testing policy theory. It is a mode of analysis sometimes designated in German-language publications as *Wirkungsforschung,* or "effect" research. A reasonable English label is product analysis. Resting often on survey research and various branches of social psychology, it is usually large-scale and ex post facto. It summarizes a set of social indicators under varying conditions of policy input to assess the overall achievements of a set of programmatic efforts.

The principal audience for product research is not the manager or administrator but the politician, the policy maker, the central planner. It is designed to test the fundamental assumptions of a broad pattern of policy. At its scientific best, it falsifies policy assumptions. It has proven often to be very threatening to policy makers and bureaucrats.

The organization of the American policy evaluation industry was best suited to the *Wirkung*/product rather than to the *Vollzug*/process model. Large contracts for national surveys or expensive experiments were more common (or at least more conspicuous; see Chapter 2) than comparable expenditures for systematic analysis of administrative procedures or feedback processes.

Evaluation contracts were often granted from central agencies, largely disassociated from the day-to-day administration of programs. The Office of Planning and Evaluation of the Department of Health, Education,

Figure 1.2 Alternative Models for Evaluation Research

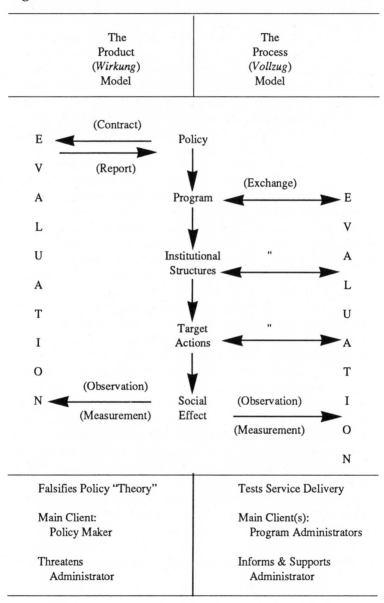

and Welfare was established, implicitly if not explicitly to provide a watchdog function over major social programs, parallel to but separate from the implementing agencies.

The cost of research, the necessity of building and maintaining an elaborate infrastructure for national surveys, data management, complex computing services, and the need to maintain highly trained personnel on "soft money" encouraged a pattern of large-scale projects. Most of the senior people in the new or expanded think tanks spent as much time writing proposals for new contracts as they did doing the research on the contracts in place. The atmosphere of such settings, though exciting, was also hectic and insecure.

Far more profit could be made from a big national survey, which would also keep a newly built field staff on the payroll, than from twenty-five case studies on information flows in regional bureaucracies. Also, the former gets more publicity than the latter. Profit came with a steady flow of new contracts. There was minimum incentive for communicating routine findings into the decision or implementation process. That was the business of bureaucrats, not of the evaluation industry.

One result was a rising mountain of rarely read or used evaluation studies. Fiscal relationships up and down the research hierarchy were refined, but horizontal linkages to responsible bureaucracies were largely unattended. The message often did not get delivered.

Unfortunately, perhaps, for the messengers, when it did get delivered, the message was not always what those who received it wanted to hear. Rather than serving as an aid to management, the cumulative lesson of policy evaluation, at least as translated through the media and the receiving instruments of policy makers, was not so much to suggest means for improved program management as to challenge the theoretical foundations of the programs. Even the conventional statistical tools of social science, such as tests of statistical significance, loaded the evidence against demonstration of positive results of policies and in favor of falsifying the hopes of policy makers.

Alas, as Aaron Wildavsky so eloquently argues, the lesson seems to be that governments are good at moving money but mostly ineffective at changing social values, behavior, or sociopolitical structures.

How did we learn that lesson? At least in part through fairly good policy evaluation.

The Unpleasant Message

Some of the most publicized evaluations showed that preschool and related special education programs had no apparent impact on either the motivation or the cognitive capacities of disadvantaged children.

The federally enforced right to vote for black people has transformed political life of many towns and cities, to the point that many black political leaders no longer advocates neighborhood racial integration lest they lose their local majority. But the Community Action Programs that provided federal funds to enhance the organizational potential of the poor are widely perceived as having accentuated rather than ameliorated antagonisms between blacks and whites in urban neighborhoods.

Job training programs for teenagers removed that group from the streets during their enrollment in the programs but had no visible positive effect on attitudes toward the world of work (Hedlund and Nachmias, 1980). Compared to general economic growth, the training was insignificant in reducing teenage unemployment.

None of the crime programs seem to have changed criminals' attitudes or behavior, although, for those who can afford them, better locks and burglar alarms seem to be fairly effective in discouraging break-ins.

Government programs have not made a noticeable dent in alcohol abuse. And changes in drug consumption patterns are unrelated to public rehabilitation programs. Restricting the supply of drugs at least prices some potential users out of the market when they cannot steal enough to sustain their habit. The old laws of supply and demand seem far more effective than the best that social psychology has to offer.

Deinstitutionalization of mental patients turned poor, disturbed people onto the streets at a time when welfare rolls of communities were already under fiscal stress. One consequence is rising homelessness.

Today's old and poor were probably poor before they got old.[3] Older people today have more money and better medical care than ever before, but it remains questionable if they are happier, especially since many remain physically alive long after their apparent capacity to enjoy life has disappeared. It has even become socially acceptable, if not fashionable, to introduce cost-benefit considerations into discussions of life maintenance.

Our water, our air, and our public places are cleaner, quieter, and less threatened than probably at any time in this century. But the cleansing has come at high cost to consumers and, perhaps, to the rate of economic growth, with much of the burden falling on the least economically advantaged people in our society. Environmental protection is apparently regressive, at least in the short run.

Perhaps sex education has enhanced physical pleasure, but illegitimate births among teenagers are soaring. More than half of the babies born in our nation's capital have no legal father. Not only have older forms of venereal disease not disappeared, but they have reached near epidemic levels on some university campuses. AIDS and herpes were unheard-of twenty years ago. Divorce rates continue to climb. And who knows if those who stay married are happier, especially as a result of sex education? Sex education in the schools seems to have contributed more to gymnastics than to personal hygiene or social values.

Bilingual education programs have disappointed their most enthusiastic supporters. It is unclear if Hispanic children are any happier for having a dual educational structure, in English and Spanish, or if they are happier simply being tossed into the English environment. It appears that the rate of English acquisition has not accelerated as a result of millions of federal dollars spent on bilingual programs.

The programs moving money from the better-off to the less-well-off continue, and there seem to be positive benefits.[4] Older people have the largest share of discretionary expenditures of any segment of the population. Unemployment is disconcerting but rarely life-threatening, given insurance and other available services.

Children born to poor, unmarried mothers rarely live in affluence but have ready access to basic medical care, to minimal sustenance, and to a level of education high by world standards, if not by the standards of the best that the West has to offer.

Not all of the bad news was brought exclusively by policy evaluators, that is, by the new social science industrialists. But the frequent message of big policy research projects tilted often in the negative or dubious direction. The policy evaluators, who were so enthusiastically in league with the proponents of social engineering and who so eagerly sought the grants and contracts, have, in effect, bitten the hand that fed them.

In large part because of the structure of the evaluation industry, I would argue, the question posed by most of the research on new social programs was not, How to do it better? but Why do it at all?

Instead of serving principally as a management tool for social programs, policy evaluation has challenged the theoretical underpinnings of those programs. To Vietnam, Watergate, and the other disillusionments of the post-Kennedy era has been added the cumulative realization of the incapacity of our policy instruments to change human values and behavior in any profound way very quickly. The message of policy evaluation has added to the "graying of America." And the expenditure patterns on social science research and development suggest that the politicians have killed the messengers.

Is the Messenger Dead or Only Wounded?

Or have they? Perhaps it is only a serious wound. Certainly the Reagan administrations did not share the hubris of the Kennedy-Johnson-Nixon years. Carter was discouraged and discouraging because of his pessimism about both the public and the private sectors. President Ronald Reagan elegantly voiced the now widely accepted skepticism about government's capacity to manage social values and behavior. But he retained and articulated a broad faith in the private economy and American moral fiber as driving forces for social growth and justice.

Those who do not accept President Reagan's faith or optimism at least seemed willing to admit to more doubt than they had a quarter of a century before about the utility of social engineering. Those who are more wedded to social *science* and less to social *engineering* may not be so disappointed as our colleagues who were earlier so optimistic about the capacity of government to manage human behavior. Social science made enormous advances under the financial and intellectual stimulus of the halcyon days of evaluation research, even though the extragovernmental industry (in universities and think tanks) subsided.

We learned a great deal about research methods and techniques. We learned how to apply modern data-collection and computing technology to long-standing dilemmas. We gained experience in the administration of research, which shows up in more efficient work in and out of the university.

Some are prepared to suggest that, if the message of evaluation research encourages conservative politicians, so be it. One wonders why, however, if the message was so conservative, the Reagan administration did not choose to increase money for social science research rather than allow the decline in federal support to continue.

The answer lies in the basic theoretical difference between the social engineers of the 1960s and the more managerial philosophy of 1980s conservatism. Policy evaluation rests on an assumption of rational decision making. If, through evaluation research and other devices, you know the consequences of alternative policy instruments, you can choose rationally which route to follow in making policy. In that sense, although the results of past research have challenged many such mechanistic assumptions, the research enterprise remains an instrument of the social rationalist. It is an engineering tool.

Modern conservatism, however, challenges the fundamental assumptions of naive rationalism (Johnson, 1983). It places high regard on the uncanny capacity of individual, ordinary people who choose to avoid or to subvert attempts at regimentation. It doubts, and often morally rejects, the ability of government programs rationally, deliberately, or dramatically to change human values and behavior. Therefore, modern conservatism has no need for such tools of rationality as evaluation research, at least not for *Wirkungsforschung*. When such research can be useful as propaganda, to show the failure of past social programs, contemporary conservatives are happy to publicize it. But the supply of past studies is more than adequate to the demand for such "killer research."

Lessons: The Potential for Process Research

Modern conservatives might well join hands with policy researchers in the development of efficient mechanisms of public management. Both the conservative skeptic and the optimistic, perhaps left-leaning, social engineer, though probably differing in measures of adequacy, have a fundamental interest in cost-effectiveness. As a consequence, support for in-house evaluation-as-management-tool has apparently been maintained at a healthy level through several years of conservative administration.

Yet, as I noted earlier, the American policy evaluation industry tended to underemphasize the process/*Vollzug* model of policy evaluation as a management tool. The development of research for effective public management, the result of process research, does not fit tidily into the large, centralized structures common in the American policy evaluation industry during its peak period. Effective process research requires rather small, routine projects, closely coordinated with practitioners. It requires attention to details of administration. It requires exploitation of the experience and wisdom of public administrators. It also requires a matching of that experience to the rigorous analytical skills and research tools of different social science disciplines. (I shall return to this theme in later chapters, especially in Chapter 7.)

The Schweizerischer Nationalfonds (Swiss National Science Foundation) has sponsored and published a series of case studies entitled *Wie wird Forschung relevant?* (How does research become relevant?). The program of case studies, described by Dieter Freiburghaus and Willi Zimmerman, provide insights that reinforce lessons from American experience (1985).

Public policy research is useful when it is applied to a current problem faced by both administrators and policy makers. It is useful when the researchers refrain from gratuitous criticism. It is useful when aimed at concrete solutions rather than ideological preaching. Research is useful when there is a basis of trust between the practitioner and the researcher. And it is useful when the recommendations for change are both specific and sensitive to the political and economic realities with which politicians and administrators must live and work.

Policy evaluation as a tool of management, rather than as a test of social theories, requires establishing regular channels of communication up, down, across, and between hierarchies. It requires short personal feedback loops between researchers and responsible practitioners, both in the center and in the field.

Perhaps the United States is simply too big for such linkages between researchers and public officials, at least at the national level. There is more to effective research than designing a survey, analyzing the data, and putting it on paper. It requires consultation between researcher and practitioner at all phases, especially in the follow-up after the research is done. Effective evaluation, as a tool for public management, does require some of the objectivity of the independent researcher. The profit motive of the private research industry is not always compatible with that independence and objectivity. Academics may be freer. But effective evaluation for improved management must also assume that the research is not a one-shot, ex post facto job, but an ongoing process. It will always require external experts, such as social scientists, if for no other reason than that active bureaucrats and policy makers do not have the time or inclination to record and catalog their own lessons or to communicate them to their peers.

An ongoing system of researcher-practitioner cooperation must rest on trust and mutual confidence and also requires some institutional capacity. Fortunately, in the Untied States, the institutional capacity of the universities for public management assistance has been damaged less than have the large think tanks (see Chapters 2 and 3).

The United States may be too big for a national system of personal yet institutionalized cooperation, but such is not the case at the state and local levels. And it is at these levels that university-based institutions continue to refine and implement routine evaluation research most successfully in close cooperation with public agencies. The beneficial results of our somewhat ill-fated history of large-scale evaluation research—improved research methods, computing facilities, infrastructure—are still in place in many universities. From the established university-government linkages, we can expect continued progress in applied research for improved public management, especially at the state and local levels.

With regard to ease of internal communication, most European countries are appropriately compared to American states. Switzerland, for example, has roughly the same population as North Carolina. Switzerland is smaller in area than forty-one of the fifty states. Yet its research infrastructure may be every bit as good as the best in the United States. The Swiss communication network between researchers and practitioners can never be matched at the national level in the United States. As the Nationalfonds' publications of Frieburgerhaus and Zimmerman (1985) make clear, lessons for effective use of policy research have already been applied by some in Switzerland.

Small is beautiful in Switzerland scientifically as well as topographically and culturally. And small may be not only beautiful but efficient as well. The example warrants closer attention to the more decentralized research models that exist elsewhere, a major theme of Chapter 2.

2

Mapping U.S. Local Policy Research

Terra Firma or Terra Incognita?

Other Western countries with fairly well-developed policy analytic infrastructures may be facing actual or potential decline comparable to the seeming fate of the U.S. industry (Wollmann, 1983). In this chapter I offer a corrective to the apparent record. I suggest that, within the realm of American state-local government and public university relationships, policy analysis training and research structures comparable to the process (*Vollzugs*) model are alive and probably well.

Training in policy analysis, as it has evolved since the mid-1960s, has become fixed within curricula that are more and more standardized for persons entering state and local (and, to a lesser extent, federal) public service. Modern research tools such as statistical training and microcomputer technology, furthermore, may so affect the modes of performance of public administrators that they will increasingly incorporate policy analytic practices into their everyday activities. These developments, however, are not visible in the scholarly research of policy analysts nested in traditional disciplinary academic units. Rather, they are taking place unostentatiously in the preprofessional curricula of public administration training programs.

Before I directly elaborate these factors, however, a comparative view will be useful. Although the curve may be bent differently, policy analysis in other Western countries may be following a pattern similar to the apparent U.S. national trend. A leading West German policy analyst has written: "After more than a decade of practicing the analysis of public policies in Germany, considerable doubts have arisen about whether and how the original expectations could be fulfilled" (Wollmann, 1983).

As I have done briefly for the United States in Chapter 1, Helmut Wollmann has fitted the changing focus and fate of policy analysis in

Germany to the early enthusiasm for and subsequent sobering with the novel policy experiments of recent decades. In the case of Germany, however, the apparent disillusionment with policy experiments and analyses of their success is linked less with the actual message, as in the United States, than with changes in national politics. Decline in the popularity of and support for academic policy research was directly associated, in Germany, with the replacement of the Social Democrats by the Christian Democrats in 1982.

A similar report comes from Britain, with the unfolding of scientific priorities under the Thatcher government (Castles, 1983). The deeper roots of policy analysis's decline, however, are comparable in several countries and do not rest exclusively on the waxing and waning of the fate of particular governing parties. The message of policy analysis has been less than a full endorsement of the optimism for ready, rational resolution of complex social problems in contemporary mixed capitalist democracies.

The task in this chapter is to address certain aspects of the U.S. policy analytic condition which I see as important and yet inadequately appreciated by policy analysts in the United States or, especially, abroad. Specifically, I focus on the development of and infrastructure for university-based local policy research and allied training practices as a piece of the map that must not be overlooked in a survey aimed toward diagnosis and prescription. It is my hope that the institutional and professional practices I discuss may constitute targets worthy of some salutary emulation. I will not, however, thoroughly diagnose the condition outside the United States to learn the extent to which the features I stress are at all malleable or exportable.

I focus here on the history and structure of subnational (state and local) policy analytic activities. My argument is that this set of activities constitutes a major, if not easily measured, component of the net productivity on the policy analysis landscape in the United States. Further, it is the locus of some of the most routinized, interactive, useful analyst-practitioner linkages on the American terrain. It is there that the process model discussed in Chapter 1 is best approximated in action.

These researcher-client linkages are attuned to the U.S. cultural and historical situation. But even though they evolved in a peculiar context, they may hold lessons for people elsewhere.

The Extension Tradition and Its Academic Role

Wollmann (1983) accurately spots the major benchmarks in the evolution of U.S. policy analytic development, often reflecting America's special penchant for pragmatism and practicality. He mentions, but does not elaborate, the land-grant college movement that began with the Morrill Act of 1862. That historic legislation established a procedure for federal support of agricultural colleges in universities, agricultural research stations, and an extension service. Thus was begun a system for research, technology development, and delivery of innovations that must have played an enormous role in the acceleration of American agricultural productivity.

Historically the Morrill Act was for U.S. education what Bismarck's social legislation was for the welfare state in Europe. The Morrill Act set up a trust fund system, based on income from the sale of public land, in each state for "at least one college where the leading object shall be, without excluding other scientific and classical studies and including military tactics, to teach such branches of learning as are related to agriculture and the mechanic arts, in such manner as the legislatures of the states may respectively prescribe, in order to promote the liberal and practical education of the industrial classes in the several pursuits and professions in life."

The U.S. practicality that Wollmann notes is noplace better expressed than in the Morrill Act. It was the means for founding many major universities, including Illinois, Minnesota, Wisconsin, Iowa State, Michigan State, Ohio State, Cornell, and others of equivalent stature. Within many of those land-grant colleges the extension model, initially set up for agricultural development, has diffused to other disciplinary areas, including government research. The model is simple in its outline, as seen in Figure 2.1.

If I want to know what variety of carrots to plant in my upstate New York garden, I call the county agricultural extension office for the latest publication on carrots. A pamphlet will be sent indicating which varieties of seeds and planting techniques have been tested most recently at the New York State Agricultural Experiment Station in Geneva, which works in close collaboration with Cornell University's college of agriculture. If I want my soil tested, I take a sample to the county extension office. When I built a pond on my land, I obtained free engineering consultation through the same office. And I am only a hobbyist, not a productive farmer.

The same land-grant universities that have been the hubs of the agricultural extension movement were also the pioneers in founding government research centers closely linked to state and local policy-making bodies. It was and continues to be a conscious policy in most of those centers to follow the extension model.

That extension model is the closest approximation in practice to *Vollzugsforschung*, as introduced in Chapter 1. Though I deliberately leave the term *basic* academic research in Figure 2.1, I do so precisely to underscore the absence of delineation or independence between "basic" and "applied" research. The rise of policy analysis in the social sciences put the final nail in the coffin of that separation. Applied research is research inspired principally by the desire to meet a need rather than by pure scientific curiosity. The product orientation is less a matter of substance or method than of modes of professionalization and routinization.

A key to the professionalization and routinization of applications in the agricultural research centers, sometimes called experiment stations, was a structure of career opportunity for researchers that was distinct

Figure 2.1 The Extension Model of Research — Application Linkages

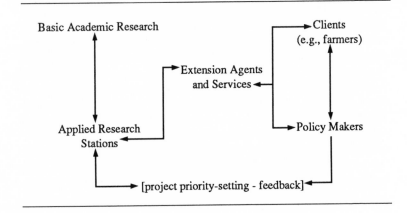

from the customary incentive system of university faculties. Customary faculty research places a high premium on originality and generality. A new, broadly applicable finding, reported in reasonably elegant rhetoric (especially in the humane sciences) gets published in national or international scholarly journals, receives commendation from peers, and yields promotion and tenure for the researcher within the academy. Cross-breeding carrots to fit the soil and climatic conditions peculiar to upstate New York is unlikely to garner such academic rewards. Cumulation, replication, and application, however, are the bywords of the Extension Service. To provide an incentive system for such work by high-quality researchers in agricultural inquiry required establishment of a "para-academic" structure. Vague analogies to such para-academic structures exist for policy analysis and public administration research.

Many students of public administration are familiar with the Hoover Commissions that studied and provided the impetus for U.S. national administrative reform in the 1940s. Less well known are the "Little Hoover Commissions" that were appointed in the years after World War II to modernize state and local governments. Commonly, these bodies had substantial representation of professors of state and local government and/or public administration from the nearby state university.

One result of the Little Hoover Commissions was the establishment or expansion of bureaus of government research in or affiliated with political science departments, especially in public universities near state capitals. In many cases, these were the progenitors or models for the multitude of institutes now surveyed in various directories (see discussion later in this chapter).

When I was in graduate school at Indiana University (circa 1960), the Bureau of Government Research, headed by a political science Ph.D. specializing in public administration, was the virtual staff arm of the state budget office. The governor's budget was sketched and largely fleshed out, as well as physically prepared, in the Indiana University bureau. When the services of persons in allied disciplines were needed, they were called from across the campus.

Today, that routine work has been professionalized within the halls of government agencies proper. The university institutes are oriented much more toward research and analysis projects and consultation than toward actual public administrative staff work. But the service linkages persist, taking on a more social science mode in the host of "institutes of public affairs" or "centers for policy analysis" that dot the U.S. academic landscape.

These state linkages and their local counterparts (larger in number but with smaller project budgets) are not cost-free for the academics involved. It is rare that a truly para-academic environment can be found for policy research and consultation in U.S. universities, with a fully developed but independent set of standards for career advancement. Extension work has commonly meant a sacrifice of "scholarly eminence."

There are notable exceptions, but the behavioral revolution in particular tended to direct political science along branches that had few roosting places for the "practitioners" from the government research centers. Yet to the extent that social science's broader theoretical results were to find their way into the policy-making realm, the extension scholars were the active transmitters.

Institutionalizing Analysis via Training and Technology

The eviction of the extensionists from the edifice of academic prestige has been partially rescinded in recent years by the emergence of *public management* and/or *policy evaluation* (not always distinguished clearly from each other). They are arenas of inquiry in which the linkage between generalizable social inquiry and useful information is forged.

A key here is the growing recognition of the methodological neutrality of contemporary policy research (Von Beyme, 1985). The tools of social science (ex ante: benefit-cost analysis, operations research, simulation; ex post: survey research, aggregate data analysis) are also the tools employed by the public administrator on the job. As the halls of decision making, at least at the staff level, are increasingly populated by young persons with their own university-based exposure to the methods of social science, these techniques become less and less a cognitive barrier between town and gown. These techniques are increasingly being incorporated into the *lingua franca* of policy assessment in both the public and the academic sectors.

Even the very "nuts-and-bolts" model public administration curriculum recommended by the National Association of Schools of Public

Affairs and Administration (NASPAA) includes at least one semester of research design and statistics. Computing skills, especially on microcomputers, using prepared library programs for management analysis, will not be long in coming to that curriculum (Renfrow and Gow, 1985).

Here one must distinguish between recruitment patterns in the European and the U.S. public sectors. The jurists' dominance of career entry on the Continent stands in stark contrast to the U.S. practice (Peters, 1978:96–98). NASPAA is aspiring, haltingly, to become in effect a professional certification agency, or at least a program accreditation entity, for the model university curriculum required for entry into the public sector. The Master's of Public Administration (MPA) or its equivalent will be the modal and model diploma (Renfrow and Gow, 1985).

We can already see the effects in the community around the State University of New York (SUNY)–Binghamton, after roughly ten years of producing students in such a program. Nearly every local agency has, in the middle to upper echelons, at least one and often several graduates of the SUNY-Binghamton program for the Master's of Arts in Public Policy and Administration. Other graduates have been placed, for example, in the U.S. Office of Management and Budget, the Research Division of the New York City Fire Department, the New York State Department of Health, and the New York State Assembly. These people now serve as links for placement of their academic successors at the entry level, freshly graduated from our program.

We regularly have special seminars in which successful graduates are brought back to the campus to address incumbent students. The universal message conveyed by the alumni to the current students (most of whom are struggling to learn statistics and data management) is that the methods sequence was the component of their academic program that proved most important on the job in a public agency.

Government computing centers and their staffs will soon be under siege. The impact of microcomputers, already in widespread use at all levels in the public sector, suggests the likelihood of a minor information revolution. Heretofore, public managerial personnel have been responsible for providing information about their agencies to a central computing facility. The computer center staff manage the data with complex, arcane, usually customized programs to produce drafts of more or less

routine reports of agency performance, indicating both financial trans-
actions and clients' traits. The responsible manager then edits and trans-
mits such reports upward, never to hear about them again, if all is well.

The manager has, therefore, little flexibility in the use or structuring
of the agency's "facts." With statistical and policy analytic training,
however, coupled with the information accessing and manipulating
power of the desktop computer, managers will increasingly "face the
facts" themselves, with a far wider range of uses to which such information can be put. These uses will include the execution, in effect, of
on-line program monitoring and evaluation.[1]

I conclude that the methodological mysticism that has stood as a
barrier to communication and use of policy inquiry on the job is being
conquered. It will be less and less necessary for the extensionist in
academia to sacrifice scholarly identity, even though that scholarly identity requires the acquisition and use of formerly arcane tools of analysis.[2]

To the extent that the myriad of government-policy-administrative
research centers are also the laboratories in which future public administrators do their apprenticeships, those persons will be not only an
audience but also a market for future applied, local research, when such
research flows from the normal needs of analytically oriented public
managers.

I conclude that one cannot forecast the market for applied, empirical
policy research without also forecasting the supply of social science–
trained public administrators. Is this an appropriate "leverage point"
for the long-term prospects of policy analysis in Europe or elsewhere?
If my analysis in Chapter 1 is valid, the greatest marginal growth will
not take place in large think tanks, doing *Wirkungsforschung,* but rather
in more localized extensionlike units. These have not been adequately
mapped for evaluation by foreign importers.

Pieces of the Map

In all likelihood, the vast majority of policy analysis projects, however
defined, escape the general attention of the academic community, not
to mention the universe of potential government clients. With no pre-
tense to comprehensive coverage, the *Policy Research Centers Direc-*

tory (Policy Studies Organization) reports on 124 such centers (1978). The *Directory of Programs in Public Affairs and Administration* lists 192 public affairs/administration graduate programs in the United States (1982). The *Professional Directory of Who's Who in Governmental Research* (Governmental Research Association, Inc., 1983) lists approximately 750 organizations engaged in government research, from ACTION—Housing, Inc., to the Wyoming Taxpayers Association.

None of these documents pretends to report on the full scope and content of actual research conducted. Escaping enumeration are many of the individual local research efforts of academics located at the more than two thousand baccalaureate-granting institutions in the United States.

In the mid-1970s, Policy Studies Associates produced the marvelously documented and cross-indexed *Policy Analysis Sourcebook for Social Programs* (1974). A significant percentage of the entries were policy studies focused at the local level. Yet that volume, too, could not approach comprehensiveness. And, alas, it had not been brought up to date as of this writing.

The National Technical Information Service (NTIS) provides computer-based access to virtually all evaluations and research documents produced under contract out of Washington. NTIS is a resource not used to its fullest. But it, too, does not tap the vast array of local projects executed through a host of nonfederal auspices. One can only guess, but it may be safely assumed that, by any index of effort, volume, or substantive scope, these local projects far exceed those funded through federal grants and contracts. (See the appendix to this chapter for a sampling from the SUNY-Binghamton Center for Social Analysis, none of which appear in the various indexes.)

The most ambitious effort to open a small window on this vast domain of research was probably the National Public Management Research Survey's (NPMRS) publication *Public Management Research Directory*. That document, issued in two volumes (1981 and 1982) abstracts information on 262 projects based in academic settings throughout the United States. Most are locally focused, but not all. The survey should not be viewed as comprehensive of the field, but it probably is more representative than any other comparable indexing effort.

The bulk of the projects surveyed were located in the disciplines of political science, economics, and business administration. "A 310-key-word descriptor index was developed for retrieving cases from the NPMRS file. These keywords were aggregated at five levels of generalization. The categories at the most general level were policy analysis, financial management, human resource management, information systems, external relations, and support services. The bulk of contemporary public management research is focused on the policy analysis and political (external relations) dimensions of management." (Note: "Policy analysis" is now a subfield of "public management.")

Noteworthy in light of the diffusion of quantitative skills in public administration training programs is the type of research design incorporated into the projects in the NPMRS survey:

> Less than 1 percent could be construed as experimental in nature, and only 7 percent can be considered quasi-experimental in the sense of using control variables in a multivariate analysis or using comparison groups. A few are inductive [sic] from game theoretic or other models (5 percent). Most are exploratory case studies (50 percent), or ex post facto analyses of public management issues (32 percent). The primary observational method for public management research is the mail or personal interview survey method (31 percent), with multiple observational methods (usually survey data and secondary source data) representing 24 percent. Although many research projects were considered predominantly qualitative in nature (24 percent), one half . . . involved using data sets available for reanalysis later by other public management researchers. Quantitative research designs are predominant in public management research (55 percent). In conclusion, it is possible that the levels of research methodologies reported here represent a growing sophistication of the field. (p. 11)

The majority of projects reported were conducted by one or another university-based institute of public affairs or public administration (e.g., Center for Public Affairs and Administration, University of Utah; Institute for Policy Research and Evaluation, Pennsylvania State University; Public Policy Research Organization, University of California–Irvine; Center for Public Affairs, University of Kansas). There were almost as many projects housed directly in academic departments of political science and/or administration.

The Local Training/Research Enterprise: Observations from Experience

I was initially trained in the early wave of the behavioral revolution, socialized in the norms of scorn for "applied" inquiry. Even the early policy analytic projects that were pursued by my generation of quantitatively oriented political scientists were consciously aimed at explaining the *process* rather than the *product* or *impact* of policy systems. Through a series of semiaccidental circumstances, I found myself in 1976 as director of a research center, which clearly needed to develop an applied, public-service-oriented policy research agenda.

My tools, brought from the fields of behavioralism, were readily adapted to a wide range of applied tasks, usually performed on contracts with state or local agencies. Our graduate students who worked on such projects never sensed a gap between their methodological or theoretical concerns and the needs of our clients. The client-driven projects did require a good deal of task orientation and timeliness, a set of stimuli generally healthy for academics in any event. It did mean that some interesting avenues of further exploration were often passed by in favor of addressing clients' specific needs. And for most of us in the center it meant production of much research that held little prospect for publication in disciplinary journals.

A major lesson learned was that there are compelling pedagogic, substantive, and market reasons for placing high priority on building university-based policy analysis services, focused on state and local government policy activities. Among the advantages are pedagogical benefits of student involvement, greater likelihood that the research will be used, healthy university public relations, and the richness of intensive versus extensive research. Student researchers benefit from interaction with the client and research target. It ensures that there is flesh on the skeletons of data.

Locally based research in the public sector can frequently be designed cooperatively with the client or target agency delivering services (see Freiburgerhaus and Zimmerman, 1985). Involvement of the client in design and execution of research provides an incentive for use of the finished research products.

However autonomous in theory, every university is also a corporate citizen of the community in which it is located. Few universities will fail to profit from a strong positive image among local policy makers/administrators.

Without in any way disparaging the value of extensive (e.g., national survey) policy research, there are distinct advantages, both for cumulative knowledge and for the student researcher's experience, in the opportunity to participate in case-intensive local inquiry. A substantial share of the problems in achieving policy effectiveness lie more in the realm of improved delivery than in policy theory. This, in turn, argues for closer attention to the details of implementation by the relevant research community. Current theory and observational techniques for improved implementation are poorly developed. Here a case could be made for controlled induction in identifying aspects of implementation amenable to improvement.

Generalizations of value for improving service delivery and for giving content to the political and administrative barriers to positive policy impact will come from close observation of real cases. Many such uses are readily available in the locality near most universities. One should not necessarily infer that the term *case analysis* indicates a call for ideographic or impressionistic methods.

Resources in support of research—libraries, office space, even computing facilities—are commonly located on university campuses and can be employed at marginal cost. Student labor is cheap, and students are frequently enthusiastic about the chance to be involved with the "real world" of public policy. With proper supervision, students often can provide more dedicated and higher-quality research project staff than likely to be found in either a private corporation or an in-home government research unit.

That infrastructure, with attendant expertise, is in place throughout the United States, usually embedded in politically powerful universities. A mapping of the American policy analysis landscape is incomplete without recognition of that terra incognita, which is nonetheless on terra firma. And the extension model warrants close scrutiny, if not emulation.

It cannot be claimed, however, that a universally applicable solution has been found for the problem of career development. That is, scholars who direct or work predominantly within the applied policy analysis domain, doing *Vollzugsforschung,* are problem cases for tenure and promotion committees, not unlike artists who exhibit paintings or musicians who perform at concerts in lieu of journal publications. Sometimes the dilemma is partially resolved in the terms of the initial appointment, whereby deans and department faculty agree ex ante that a particular appointee will be assessed according to extension service standards. Rarely, however, is such a solution wholly satisfactory to all parties.

My own observations of policy analysis and/or public administration research environments abroad, however, suggest that engagement in routine relationships with the public sector are not only approved but actually encouraged outside the United States. As noted in Chapter 1, with reference to Switzerland, the small size of the policy encourages such relationships. In addition, in smaller countries, the audience for more "scholarly" social inquiry (i.e., original, generalizable, and aimed exclusively at a "scientific" clientele) is less attractive, if for no other reason than the limited size of the scientific community (especially in languages less commonly used in international scientific discourse). If one is to sell an adequate number of books, they must be bought by someone other than one's academic peers.

One lesson, therefore, for European and other branches of the craft is to cling to those healthy lines of communication that exist between the academy and public agencies and to resist erecting any higher barriers in the interest of scientific "purity." Such wariness against estrangement may counter certain centrifugal forces present in the United States.

There is a centrifugal tendency of policy analysis and public administration research to spin off quasi-independent institutes, wherein applied research and training are duly recognized. Creation of.networks of such institutes, likewise, has advanced a national personnel marketplace and publication outlets that promote mutual recognition of the substance and merit of applied public policy and administration research.

One result, however, has been to stretch the lines of communication between those engaged in original, generalizable policy and administrative inquiry, on one hand, and those producing detailed, rich, cumulative replications, on the other.

The lessons to be derived form the U.S. local policy analysis map, therefore, are both negative and positive. Appreciation of this mixed message may be enhanced by attention to a few specific projects, the subject of Chapter 3.

Appendix: A Sample of Local Policy Projects Executed by the SUNY-Binghamton Center for Social Analysis

RESIDENT RELOCATION FOR THE NEW YORK STATE VETERANS' HOME, OXFORD, NY: PRE- AND POST-RELOCATION PROFILES

The Veterans' Home was faced with problems involved in moving elderly residents from accustomed quarters in an old facility to a brand-new site. Research on similar experiences in other places indicated that such a relocation could have dangerous results. The Center for Social Analysis (CSA), with participating political science, nursing, and medical school faculty, developed a plan for managing the move with the least possible disruption to the residents and also for evaluating the effects of the change in surroundings through a series of postrelocation surveys. Graduate students in political science and from the School of Nursing were involved in interviewing residents of the home, designing survey instruments, analyzing data, writing reports, and consulting with staff of the home. The project exemplifies cooperation between multiple units of the university and a community agency, with a direct benefit to the elderly residents of the home. It was funded by the New York State Department of Health.

VALIDATING THE CITY OF NEW YORK'S PROBATION RISK ASSESSMENT INSTRUMENT

New York City's Department of Probation instituted a new program of differential supervision for probationers and selected a risk-assessment instrument in use elsewhere to determine the proper level of supervision for each probationer. The CSA, using complex multivariate statistical techniques, was able to determine how well the instrument worked and if it could be improved. The study resulted in a recommendation for a new, simpler instrument with greater predictive power.

MANAGEMENT INFORMATION SYSTEM FOR THE BROOME COUNTY OFFICE FOR THE AGING

The Office for the Aging has been expanding its range of services as well as the number of clients receiving services. The staff had recognized a need for improved information management, especially of client and service records, given the wide range of services provided. Under a contract with the OFA, staff of the CSA assessed the agency's information needs, evaluated commercial information management packages, and designed improved processes. This study showed the lack of need for an expensive management information system and the possibility of a modest, locally constructed set of procedures. It involved faculty from the CSA, students and faculty from the School of Management, and staff of the University Computer Center. Recommendations were made for design of information reporting forms and a system of computerized data processing. This is an example of a project that not only prevented excessive public expenditure but also provided a learning experience for students from a program (management) who would not otherwise have been introduced to studies related to aging.

YOUTH NEEDS ASSESSMENT

The Broome County Youth Bureau is responsible for setting priorities, funding programs, and monitoring services for the twenty-seven thousand young people of the county. The CSA, working with the bureau, designed and executed a comprehensive needs assessment survey, using multistage cluster samples to enable the bureau to identify the problems and preferences of eight subgroups of the population (e.g., rural junior high school boys). The results have given the Youth Bureau an objective and reliable basis upon which to plan and evaluate programs more effectively.

RIDERSHIP SURVEY FOR BROOME COUNTY TRANSIT AUTHORITY

For five consecutive years, the CSA faculty and graduate research assistants conducted an "on-board" survey of bus riders for the local transit system. The data enabled the Transit Authority to assess accurately its progress in planning and operating an effective service, from advertising and scheduling through bus cleanliness and driver courtesy.

STATE ASSUMPTION OF THE FEDERAL COMMUNITY DEVELOPMENT PROGRAM FOR SMALL CITIES

As New York State considered its option to assume responsibility from the U.S. Department of Housing and Urban Development for the Small Cities Program, the CSA worked with the state's Housing Finance Agency to develop a workable administrative plan for takeover and management of the program, with particular emphasis on timing, staffing, and operational costs.

USING TAX-EXEMPT BONDS TO SUPPORT STATE STUDENT LOAN PROGRAM

The CSA worked with the State of New York Mortgage Agency (SONY-MA) to review and assess the options for issuing tax-exempt bonds to support an in-state student loan program in the face of likely cuts in federally guaranteed loans. CSA studied the history of federally guaranteed student loans, detailed the current programs and how they operate in New York State, analyzed the use of tax-exempt bonds for federally guaranteed and alternative loan programs in other states, and described the past, present, and future demand for loans among New York State residents. By assembling this information into a set of recommendations backed by data, CSA enabled the SONY-MA Board of Directors to make more informed policy choices.

BROOME COUNTY'S ELDERLY: A NEEDS ASSESSMENT SURVEY FOR THE OFFICE FOR THE AGING

This study, directed by political science faculty and research assistants, replicated similar surveys conducted nationally and in other communities to identify needs of older residents. It was designed as an aid to program planning and evaluation needs of the Office for the Aging. A survey was administered to a random sample of the county's elderly residents. Results for expressed need for services, in particular areas of personal and community life, were compared with each other and with national figures. The results were most interesting in demonstrating that this particular community could not be assumed to have the same priority of perceived needs as were guiding policy from Washington, based on national average figures.

PATTERNS AND DIETARY CONSEQUENCES OF PARTICIPATION BY THE ELDERLY IN A SUBSIDIZED LUNCH PROGRAM

This study was a collaborative effort involving the Medical School, the School of Nursing, and the CSA and was funded by a private foundation. Graduate students in nursing and political science conducted interviews with elderly individuals, half of whom were participants in a hot lunch program (jointly funded by the federal government and the county) and the other half of whom were nonparticipants. The data allowed evaluation of the social impact of participation, the dietary consequences for those using the service, and the consumers' satisfaction with the program. It provided an evaluation, at the local level, of a federally funded human service program. In particular, it assessed the extent to which the program was reaching target populations and the extent to which variations in the program had consequences for clients.

HEALTHY LIFESTYLE FOR SENIOR CITIZENS

Through this project, a health improvement program was provided to an experimental group of senior citizens with pre- and posttest evaluation based on indicators such as weight, blood pressure, joint flexibility, self-esteem, and life satisfaction. The project was conducted by a staff including students and faculty from the Medical School, the School of Nursing, and the Department of Political Science. Funding was provided by the local branch of Catholic Charities.

3

Testing Common Sense and Recognizing Patterns

Examples from Services for the Elderly

In the everyday world, how does process research begin? How are relationships between analysts and program personnel developed and/or damaged? What purposes are served by quantitative research, statistics, and computerized analyses in more or less routine public program evaluation in tandem with implementation (*Vollzugsforschung*)? Two purposes stand out:

Testing Common sense:
Do programs out in the field *really* fit the purposes hoped for by their supporters and administrators? At what cost, directly and in side effects?

Pattern Recognitions:
How can we sort through the murky complexity of society and everyday human relations? How can we see the patterns that will help policy makers reduce their ignorance in trying to alleviate human problems through public programs?

Formal theory provides guidance and incentive for the scientist through a set of statements about relationships from which hypotheses can be derived for test in empirical circumstances. By implication, Chapter 2 suggests that much of applied policy analysis is not very theoretical, in the sense that it is derived not from scientifically stated postulates, aimed toward maximum generalizability, but rather is inspired by clients' needs and local conditions. But I have also argued in favor of the scientific "respectability" of such "atheoretical" research. Clients' needs and local conditions provide the incentive and guidance for policy analysis. I question, however, whether the results derived from research so motivated are any less coherent or generalizable than

38

those stimulated by scientifically loftier frameworks. I further suspect that much of the "theoretical" framing in the social sciences is retro-fitted to research stimulated by considerations at least as mundane as clients' needs and local conditions.

Reports of social research usually become self-consciously theoretical at about the point at which the author runs out of data. And the result is more rhetoric than science. Why? I am not sure. But I suspect it is because of the partiality and artificiality of the way social scientists denote their domains (or "guilds"). To expect a "theory of public policy" is probably about as sensible as to expect a "theory of eating." The acts studied are not suitable to self-standing, coherent theory, in the proper philosophy of science sense. But the form and consequences of eating habits are interesting as they fit into the larger biological system. So are the patterns and consequences of public programs in-teresting as they fit into the larger social system.

What does empirical policy research do that is respectable if it does not deliberately or directly build "theory"? It tests common sense, and it aids pattern recognition.

The testing of common sense by empirical research occasionally shows that conventional wisdom is right. Sometimes it shows that com-mon sense is simply wrong. More often, however, empirical research reveals a world that is much more complex than one is led by accepted explanations to believe. Likewise, once complexity is perceived, it is helpful to have a map, some means to recognize patterns, to help the wise policy maker approach goals more efficiently.

These are important but modest mandates for empirical policy re-search. But they are eminently more realistic and useful than pretending to "build theory" or to "explain" to the ill-informed how the world actually works, especially when the "ill-informed" are seasoned policy makers and program managers.

Testing Common Sense

The "easy" sciences (e.g., physics and chemistry) are able to create, in the laboratory, circumstances that exclude impurities that would con-fuse observations. One or a few tests of expectations with purified chemicals or physical material are sufficient to deal with a hypothesis.

Unfortunately, such purity of conditions is rare in the "hard" (i.e., difficult) sciences (e.g., political science, anthropology, economics, sociology). There, we often compensate for impurity by examining very large numbers of cases, which allows us to control for alternative causes or impurities. That accounts for the frequency with which policy evaluators use survey research or other information resources to produce large numbers of observations.

A typical question from policy analysis would be, To what extent is a public program that was designed to reduce some undesirable event actually responsible for an observed reduction in that event? Suppose a government has a program to inoculate children against a particular disease. If the incidence of that disease declines, most people would give credit to the government program.

Yet, when we look (either directly or through some sort of printed record) at people in the society, it is unclear if there is a relationship between inoculation and disease, especially for diseases that are relatively rare. People who were immunized stay healthy. But people who have not been immunized through a public program also stay healthy. Some may have a natural immunity. Some may have obtained inoculation through private sources. Some may never have been exposed to the disease. Some may simply be lucky. The people we see have many different characteristics, some of which may be factors in their getting or not getting ill.

Furthermore, it may be the case that people with only a particular set of social values or characteristics (e.g., level of knowledge about health, lack of religious scruples regarding vaccination, lack of objection to a "socialist" program) will enroll in a public inoculation program.

Only by gathering much data on many people with and without illness, people who participated in vaccination programs and those who did not, and finally people with a variety of potentially relevant social attributes, can we begin to control for the impurities in our observations. Only with such information is it possible to test the commonsense assumption that an inoculation program is responsible for a difference in the frequency of a particular disease.

Common sense suggests that it cannot be healthy to wrap dried leaves in paper, place them in the mouth, set them afire, and then suck the smoke into one's lungs. Yet millions of people do just that every day in spite of the commonsense stupidity of it. And it required hundreds of thousands of cases before the health research community was able to establish convincingly that there is a positive statistical relationship between cigarette smoking and lung cancer. Most smokers do not contract lung cancer. Some nonsmokers do. But that the relationship is there can no longer be denied now that sufficient data have been collected and analyzed.

With the aid of certain techniques of quantitative research (e.g., random sampling, survey research) we are able to select a population with the necessarily wide range of impurities so that we can test the extent to which a policy experiment (inoculation of children) had the hoped-for impact (immunity from the disease).

Likewise, relatively sophisticated statistical devices are necessary in order to sort through all of the variables that exist in our sample and might obscure the real relationship we expect to find.

Pattern Recognition

Much scientific progress is based on fortunate discoveries, on seeing patterns that previously were not obvious. Sometimes while investigating one thing, an analyst discovers something else. In English, we call this fortunate but nonetheless intelligent process ''serendipity.''

During World War II, it was gradually noted that certain soldiers had unusual brown stains on their teeth but those who had a particular type of stain practically never had dental cavities. Then it was discovered that a very large number of such soldiers came from a particular community in Texas. Simplifying considerably, it was ultimately discovered that the water in that community contained minute tracings of fluoride. That discovery led to the process of fluoridation to prevent tooth decay.

With some insight into social processes, and the valuable aid of modern computing and data management tools, we can multiply our ability to identify patterns in large volumes of social, economic, and political data. Today, with such aids, we are able quickly to follow out hunches or bright guesses, a process which in former eras would have been prohibitive in time and effort.

Many different tools fit into such a kit. Space satellite photography and surveying techniques promise many major advances in natural resource preservation, weather prediction, and agricultural planning (especially in the Third World). The key is the ability to manage tremendously large amounts of data to observe patterns not formerly revealed. Often, such large data observational activities are undertaken without very good advance ideas about what might be found.

Policy analysts sometimes employ similar processes to identify the correlates of social programs.

In this chapter, I discuss a few policy evaluations that employed quantitative, statistical, computerized analysis in varying forms. These evaluations ask two questions about social services for the elderly: Did the program achieve its expected effect? What additional effects (beneficial or harmful) did the program have? In the course of the discussion, I hope to show how these studies served to test common sense and to aid in recognition of patterns.

Social Services for the Aged

What goals are sought through social services for old people? We can identify at least two major categories, with several subsidiaries in each.

Major Goal #1:
  Elderly people should be protected against avoidable physical misfortune.
    Subsidiary Goals:
      Access to high-quality health care
      Adequate housing
      Adequate diet
      Sufficient income for life necessities
Major Goal #2:
  The elderly should maintain dignified, independent, and rewarding lives, accommodated to their physical and mental conditions.
    Subsidiary Goals:
      Avoidance of loneliness; opportunities for social interaction and recreation
      Proper institutional care when conditions require it

I take no personal position on the wisdom of such normative goals. Different cultures have different values about how their elderly should be treated, ranging from reverence to avoidance. Likewise, I take no position on the relative merits of public sector versus private provision of services to the elderly. I can, however, report that such major and subsidiary goals are clearly stated in national, state, and local legislation throughout the United States. I can further report that specific programs and structures of services have been put in place, accelerating after the mid-1960s.

Especially after 1965, with the enactment under President Johnson of the Older Americans Act, there was a proliferation of community-based services for the elderly: multiservice senior citizens' centers, home nutrition (Meals on Wheels) and nursing care, subsidized access to public transportation, expanded nursing home facilities for those requiring full-time care, and publicly assisted housing projects.

The Older Americans Act of 1965 established the national Administration on Aging (AoA), which gives grants to states and communities for providing a wide range of services to the elderly. Substantial choice regarding the level, type, and mix of services to be provided is left to the communities. National guidelines are very broad, and control is minimal within those broad guidelines. Additional funds can be obtained by a locality, upon application, for planning and program evaluation. Funds may also be used for what is called "outreach," which translates as advertisement of services by the local agency so as to expand its clientele of service users. In my community one can see television advertisements for senior centers and other services of the local Office for the Aging. The local agency's budget is a function of its ability to build a clientele of elderly "customers."

In the later 1970s, the SUNY-Binghamton Center for Social Analysis conducted various studies for the Broome County Office for the Aging and for other public agencies with elderly clients. Over the years, it has been the practice of SUNY-Binghamton faculty members teaching public policy and administration to invite key policy administrators from the community to talk to students about their services. I had occasion to invite the director of the Office for the Aging, and we struck up an acquaintance. I mention these personal aspects because I believe they show something of the day-to-day features of the linkage between researchers and policy makers or administrators, which is essential to process research.

During his appearance before my class, I asked him first to describe his services. He mentioned nutrition, housing, senior centers, visiting nurse, and the like. I asked him to tell us how he and his colleagues were able to determine the degree of impact or effectiveness their programs had on the quality of life of elderly people in our community.

The director's answer was that they "guess" and "hope" that they are having a positive impact. I suggested that if we cooperated, we could do better than by guessing and hoping. We could do an evaluation that would give him an improved base for assessing the performance of his programs.

Evaluating the Hot Lunch Program

During several informal conversations between the director, some of the graduate students in the SUNY program, one or two colleagues, and me, we drew up a list of questions that might yield useful answers, if good research could be done. The director's major worry was about the effectiveness of a very expensive hot lunch program (Cingranelli et al., 1981).

Every day during the week, the Office for the Aging serves a very nice lunch in each of seven sites located in various parts of the county, some in the city, some in rural areas. Transportation is provided for those who request it. Several hundred elderly people come each day. The lunches are supervised by a nutritionist.

As a matter of policy, there is no test of who can come as long as they claim to be over fifty-five years of age. A donation box is near the door, and it is recommended that participants donate seventy-five cents, but no one monitors the donations. In practice, about as much is donated as is expected, but the meals cost much more than is collected, requiring a very large subsidy.

The sites where the lunches are served vary considerably. One is the basement of a rural church. Some, however, are multiple-purpose senior citizen centers, with recreational facilities such as billiard tables, sewing and knitting rooms, table tennis, and card tables. In addition, at regular intervals, health services are provided (for example, blood pressure checks) at the sites. Some of the sites are located in pleasant neighborhoods. Others are in semi-industrial, rather poor neighborhoods. Some of the buildings look very nice. Some are rather shabby.

The director of the program had several questions about the program's impact:

- Who participates? That is, although the program deliberately applies no test of financial need to participants, was it reaching those most in need? Some persons had noted the presence of Mercedes and other fancy cars in the parking lots. Were the poor of the county being reached?
- What could be done to maximize the participation by the poorer people of the county? Were the transportation services adequate? Did the attractiveness or location of the sites make a difference in patterns of participation?
- Did the lunch program attract people to come for other services, for example, health checkups and recreation?
- How satisfied were the participants with the program, the service, the setting, and the quality of food?

To this list of questions posed by the program director, the Center for Social Analysis staff added, after consultation with the director, a series of other questions:

- What social or psychological characteristics or personal values distinguished participants from nonparticipants?
- Did participants have different political values from those who did not participate? That is, was the service considered "welfare" and therefore objectionable to more politically conservative older people?
- Did the socioeconomic and particularly the ethnic composition of neighborhoods affect the pattern of participation? (Our county has several neighborhoods with heavy concentrations of first- and second-generation Italians, Yugoslavs, Czechs, and Poles. Did members of those groups prefer to attend senior citizen centers in neighborhoods of their own ethnic composition, or were they willing to mix with many different ethnic groups?

And finally, the most difficult question of all, which was posed by the research team and supported by the program staff:

- What impact did participation in the program have on the actual nutrition of the elderly? Did elderly persons who attended the hot lunch program have more nutritious diets than those who did not use the program?

It should be emphasized that neither the research nor the program staff had definite answers to these questions before the research was conducted. Although staff could observe, informally, some of the characteristics of those who came to the senior centers, it was not possible systematically to compare them to those who did not come. Many of those who showed up for lunch were clearly not wealthy, and some were visibly poor. But such impressions are misleading. Furthermore, without systematically observing nonparticipants, it was not possible to get an accurate picture of the difference made by the program.

With the active support and endorsement of the director of the Office for the Aging, we obtained funds from various sources to support a survey of the elderly, designed to address these questions. We saved some money by using elderly people from the community as interviewers. These people came through a part-time jobs program also sponsored by the Office for the Aging.

The study had to be based on a matched sample of participants and nonparticipants. We built a list from which to draw the sample of participants by having persons attending the lunches sign up over a period of several weeks. But to get a sample of nonparticipants was much more difficult.

It was necessary, first, to draw a random sample of households in the county, using the telephone book. According to the telephone company, 92 percent of Broome County's households have telephones, with nearly all of those without being students. Then we called that sample of nearly twelve thousand to ask if anyone over sixty years old lived in the house. We then had to ask if the elderly resident attended the hot lunch program. We thus acquired a sample of fifteen hundred households with elderly residents who did not attend the program. They constituted our nonparticipant sample frame.

We then collected data personally from participants and nonparticipants. First, we had a battery of survey questions, implicit in the research questions decided upon earlier. Second, we gave each respondent a three-day dietary record, along with verbal and written instructions on how to complete it.

The dietary record required that each respondent record on a form everything he or she ate, including the butter on toast, and an approximation of the quantity. They were also given a telephone number to call in the event of difficulty with the record. At the end of the three days, the diet forms were picked up by one of our survey staff. The contents were reviewed with the respondent to ensure accurate completion.

The survey data were transformed into computer-readable form. We had to devise a special computer program to transform the diet records into measures of sixteen basic nutrients, iron, vitamins, protein, and so on. In construction of that program, we had to borrow from around the university campus the services of nutritionists, computer programmers, and others.

The total project, therefore, incorporated data resulting from the participant survey, the nonparticipant survey, an expert assessment of the attractiveness and features of lunch program sites, demographic data from the census on neighborhood traits, measures of transportation services, and the dietary records. The results were interesting. They did not always confirm common sense. Likewise, they revealed certain patterns we would not have seen merely through everyday experience.

WHO PARTICIPATES?

The hope and expectation was that poorer people would take greater advantage of the program. Generally, the participants did come from the lower-middle income range. But, unfortunately, and initially mysteriously, the very poorest elderly, even though physically able, did not participate.

A few well-off people participated. They were the ones with the Mercedes. But they also provided transportation for others not so well off. And, after all, how many older Americans get to ride in a Mercedes?

The view of the agency staff was that some socioeconomic mix was probably good for the program because it made it look less like a charity operation. One should not immediately condemn such post-hoc rationalization of program goals. In a sense, it is the program administrator's equivalent of structural functionalism: if it is there and it seems to work, what purpose is it serving? (The American fifty-five-mile-per-hour speed limit was originally imposed to save oil. After several years of experience, it was very unclear how much oil was saved, but the annual saving of thousands of lives was virtually undeniable.)

The socioeconomic characteristics of participants were unrelated to such traits of the setting as the attractiveness of the site, the neighborhood location, or even the proximity or access to transportation. This proved to be an important finding because the agency was seriously considering major investments in physical facilities in poorer neighborhoods to expand participation by poorer people. It was a surprise to learn that the attributes of the facility were irrelevant, and that finding guided future planning.

SIDE EFFECTS

The luncheon program did serve to get people to take advantage of other services, which they would not have used were it not for the meal. These included, for example, health checkups and recreation.

SATISFACTION

When asked why they participated, most people said: "Because it's a good, cheap lunch, although they serve too much cabbage." Cabbage aside, the level of satisfaction was very high.

These findings were both interesting and useful to the Office for the Aging. But the staff was puzzled that the very poorest (about 10 percent of the elderly residents of the county) were nearly absent from the luncheon program.

The questions the research staff added to the inventory also yielded interesting results, which helped clarify some of the questions raised above.

VALUES, SOCIAL AND PSYCHOLOGICAL FEATURES

Participants and nonparticipants were virtually identical in distribution of political attitudes. Political conservatives participated as much as more left-leaning folks. The program was not considered welfare, especially because it provided the opportunity to pay through donation. (At the request of the director of the program, we did not inquire about the frequency or amount of money people donated to the program.) But it seemed more than that. Somehow services for the elderly, except for specific money support through local welfare services, are not perceived as socialism, even by otherwise very conservative old people.

Ethnic composition of the neighborhood had no effect on patterns of participation. Our community has a very small black population so that was not a factor. Comparable studies elsewhere have shown a reluctance of the elderly to enter a neighborhood predominantly of the opposite race. One of the findings that surprised the agency personnel was that many participants circulated regularly, attending a different site on different days merely for variety.

In our interviews we asked a number of questions about patterns of social activities such as church, clubs, and political party activity. These questions were not suggested by the director or other agency personnel but were added by the ivory-tower social scientists. And they yielded one of the most important findings of the survey. The most important single variable differentiating the participants from the nonparticipants was a past history of organized community activity. Those who had always been active in community groups were far more likely to take advantage of the lunch program.

This was a case of pattern recognition in the data analysis. After noting this relationship, we went back to the data and examined the extent of group activity of the very poorest people, those about whom we worried most because the program did not reach them. As we might now expect, we found that the poorest of the nonparticipants seldom participated in groups. They were lonely, isolated, and sometimes probably antisocial people. They had been that way all their lives. And now it was having a sad impact on their well-being.

This finding seems to have led to an increased effort on the part of the agency to publicize the luncheon program and the transportation services in those parts of the community where the poorest people are most frequently to be found. The agency also arranged with the welfare office to distribute information and to urge poorer people to take advantage of the program. Later informal observations suggested that these efforts bore some fruit.

Dietary Impact

We all know old people who do not seem to eat as well as they should. One of the major motivations of the designers of the lunch program nationally was the impression that diets of the elderly were often nutritionally deficient. Our analysis of the dietary records, however, showed no difference in the diets of participants and nonparticipants. Those who prepared their own meals at home received as much essential nutrition as those who went to the hot lunch programs, except, again, for the very poor. We cannot, of course, be sure that the act of keeping the record did not have some residual effect on the meal planning of people during the period of the study. But, at a minimum, it was not consistent with the expectations of common sense.[1]

Interestingly, the reaction of the director of the agency was unexciting. He said that, though surprised, he was not bothered by the lack of nutritional impact. It is worth the cost, he said, to get these people out and to provide them the chance for social contact and a little fun. Fair enough—but might there be a less costly way to achieve that result?

Needs Assessment

The support of the director was sufficient for us to get another research contract, this time paid by the county legislature. This project was what is commonly labeled a "needs assessment." It shows how researchers can sometimes get in political trouble (Ingraham and Hofferbert, 1981).

Presumably, an elaborate set of programs for a particular public ought, rationally, be related somehow to the needs of that public. Although broad choice was left by the Older Americans Act, it did contain some requirements for program planning. The national AoA had recommended that each local program periodically conduct a needs assessment of the elderly in its community. Survey designs and pretested questionnaires could be obtained from the AoA in Washington. Nothing was required about the research design or about the uses to which the assessment should be put once it was conducted. But since it was recommended by the AoA, the director requested money from the county legislature for the Center for Social Analysis to do a survey.

It was a simple survey, which could be conducted by telephone.

Basically, it asked a series of standardized questions (previously asked in a national sample survey conducted by the AoA). The questions asked elderly respondents how satisfied they were with their housing, the transportation facilities of their neighborhood, access to and quality of health care, recreational facilities, their income, and what services they wanted from the Office for the Aging.

National studies had shown that, across the country, an average of about 70 percent of the elderly expressed satisfaction with their housing, transportation, health care, and recreational facilities. About 45 percent were satisfied with their income.

Now we come to the political aspect of our study. The same director with whom we had cooperated on the hot lunch study had contracted with our center to do the needs assessment survey. Between signing the contract and reporting the study results, however, there were local elections which resulted in a change of party in the county government. The director of the Office for the Aging, a political appointee, was replaced. So it was to the new director that we made our final report on the needs assessment.

Unfortunately for our research budget, we discovered that the elderly of Broome County, New York, are an incredibly satisfied lot of people. (No Florida for me when I retire; I am going to stay right here in Broome County.) Compared to 70 percent satisfaction with transportation, housing, and health care nationally, over 90 percent of our respondents were satisfied. Seventy percent were even satisfied with their income, compared to 45 percent nationally. And, most damaging, few of them expressed any need for, knowledge of, or desire for services from the Office for the Aging. Because the county legislature, which provides much of the budget of the Office for the Aging, was paying for our research, we had to report our findings to the legislature. We reported that the elderly of Broome County were very content, thank you very much. And despite efforts to soften our language, we could not disguise the fact that they did not want or apparently need much from the Office for the Aging.

But before making the report generally available to persons outside the Office for the Aging, we followed customary procedure in the center and invited the client to comment on a draft report. That invitation resulted in a very vigorous exchange in which we accepted full responsibility for the study, deleted any references to or acknowledgment of assistance from agency staff, and entered a series of (appropriate but rather gratuitous) qualifiers about the nature of the data, the threats to the validity of the evidence, and so on. Although no apparent damage was done to its budget, that was our last contract with the Office for the Aging. This piece of process research ended the research process.

The Oxford Home Study

There is one more instructive example in the realm of services for the elderly that we conducted for another agency. This was a project for the state Department of Health rather than for the local Office for the Aging.

In the small town of Oxford, New York, the State Department of Health maintains a special residential and nursing home for military veterans and their family members. In 1979, it was home for about 180 very elderly people, mean age eighty-two years. The facility was a nineteenth-century structure, with three floors, each consisting of one long hallway, along which facilities and individual residents' rooms were arrayed. It had very high ceilings and generally gave the impression of a cross between a prison and a hospital. Most visitors and staff found it depressing and apparently inefficient. Charles Addams would have admired the old house.

In the mid-1960s a group of architects, gerontologists, and social psychologists from Cornell University was commissioned to design a "state-of-the-art" facility, incorporating the best of existing knowledge and informed speculation on the relationship between architecture, aging, and facilities management. That team produced a plan for a "modular" structure, with groups of ten to twelve two-resident, two-room suites opening onto a common area, with television, lounge facilities, and spaces for visitors for each of the modules. Nursing stations would be decentralized, with administrative centers, dining rooms, and a small shopping center in the middle of the entire complex. Outside, adjacent to each living module, vegetable and flower gardens would be provided for the residents, raised so that they could be worked from wheelchairs and so that ambulatory gardening residents would not have to bend over.

The floors of the halls were to be made of a textured brick surface, on the theory that elderly people are insecure walking on smooth surfaces and are also likely to slip and fall on them. If they could feel a slightly irregular floor surface beneath their feet, they were expected to be more willing to walk about.

The shopping complex would have a beauty shop, snack bar, and a place for people to buy small gifts for their visitors (assuming that many residents would like to present gifts to their grandchildren and great-grandchildren). Small stores would also stock and sell handicraft items for residents to purchase for their hobbies. Classes in handicrafts would be conducted in special facilities. There were also a small sports area and recreational facilities.

One can readily see the theory behind this design. The old facility was presumed to induce anonymity. The few facilities it had were split on three floors. They were distant from many residents. Acoustics were dreadful. One could often hear mentally ill and physically suffering people crying and moaning.

The new facility would create an atmosphere conducive to independence, easy interaction, and diversification of activity. The basic objective was to ensure that the elderly residents would have maximum opportunities for activity and independence within their physical and mental means.

One source of concern on the part of the management before the move to the new facility was to avoid "relocation trauma." Research had shown that previous efforts to move large numbers of fragile old people often increased mortality rates dramatically, both at the time of the move and in subsequent weeks as they found themselves unable to adjust to new surroundings. Relocation trauma means the chance that the move would kill a few of the people.

The Center for Social Analysis was asked to develop a relocation plan that took account of the existing research and fitted it to the conditions of the Oxford Home. In other words, we were not actually to conduct original research, but rather to serve as expert reviewers and translators. The CSA staff, however, saw an additional opportunity for useful research. Given the elaborate social science and architectural hypotheses that were embodied in the new home, we proposed to do a time-series study testing the impact of the new home on the activity patterns and general sense of life quality among the residents. The administrators of the home readily agreed, and a contract was let.

In collaboration with a gerontologist from a neighboring university, as well as nursing faculty and students, we exhaustively searched the literature on relocation trauma. On the basis of that synthesis of relatively complex research (the technology of which would not have been clear to the staff of the home), we designed a relocation plan that anticipated avoiding as much trauma as possible for the residents. It consisted of a few simple steps. Each resident would be shown the plans and arrangement of the new home, and they would be given as much choice as possible as to which apartment they would get. In the few weeks before the move, each resident who was physically able was taken to the new home (only two hundred meters away) and encouraged to take some possessions to put in the new apartment.

The literature had suggested that anxiety and fear of uncertain conditions was a major factor in relocation trauma. With help from the CSA staff, a Move Committee of the residents was formed to assist in planning and counseling. Finally, although it was not explicit in any of the prior research, it seemed that one factor in relocation trauma was that residents often did not sleep the night before a move because of their level of excitement and anxiety. Therefore, for any residents who had a history of difficulty sleeping, sleeping pills were administered the night before the move.

CSA research staff were present before, during, and immediately after the move, principally providing help with the extra work associated with the move, but also to be alert for unforeseen events or problem-causing circumstances. The result was very encouraging. We were unable to detect any increase in illness, psychological reactions, or deaths above average at the time or in the weeks following the move.

But the project had two phases. Not only were we interested in minimizing relocation trauma, we were also engaged in research to test the impact of the new facility of the residents' activity levels and satisfaction. To accomplish this latter purpose, we executed an elaborate survey of all of the physically capable residents. The form of the survey is what is commonly labeled a panel study, that is, a survey of the same persons at sequential time points to determine changes in behavior or attitudes. The data management problems of panel studies are severe but easily managed with appropriate computing and programming facilities, which were already available in standard form. The first wave of the survey, to provide baseline data, was executed in the weeks before the move. It was repeated one month after the move and then one year later.

Panel studies often encounter problems in that people interviewed on the first wave move or otherwise cannot be located for subsequent waves of the study. The more waves of the study, the higher the "panel mortality," as the reduction in number of respondents is called. In the panel study of residents of the Oxford Home, there was no problem with locating respondents in subsequent waves, but there was very specific panel mortality, in that about 15 percent of the home's residents die each year.

The principal objective of the panel study was to detect the extent to which levels of activity and general satisfaction improved with the new facility. We employed graduate nurses as interviewers. They had to be specially trained to interview this vulnerable population. In the interviews we inquired about a wide range of residents' activities. We also asked about friendship patterns and frequency of collective activities with others, a variation of network analysis. Finally, in the interviews in the new home, we asked about use of and satisfaction with specific and general conditions.

The findings proved very interesting, and, alas, somewhat disappointing for the designers of the new home. There were some changes in particular types of activities. For example, some residents did use the new gardens and recreational facilities. But the general level of social interaction actually dropped.

Friendship patterns and networks in the old home were broken up and did not reform in the new home. Apparently, the long halls in the old home, in contrast to the modular arrangement in the new one, actually encouraged broad social interaction. Many residents, even those in wheelchairs, would often sit in the hall outside their door in the old home, where they could observe and, at least vicariously, take part in all that went on. In the new modular structure, they tended to stay in their rooms and watch television. Residents who had difficulty getting along with each other had been able to avoid intense contact in the old home. In the new one, proximity magnified such interpersonal problems.

Staff members also reported that it was more difficult to supervise and watch over the residents in the new structure. It proved inconvenient to decentralize nursing and staff services to the various modules because it was impossible to anticipate the mix of services needed. Many specialized staff found themselves walking much of the time from one module to another at the opposite end of the home.

Even the new textured floor received a negative evaluation. The residents found it disturbing, and they had a fear of tripping, which discouraged walking about the home. Some residents who did walk about would get lost and had to be led back to their own module.

Our surveys did, inadvertently, discover some new needs that could be met. For example, many of the men in the home expressed a strong desire for a cocktail hour. The rules prohibited alcoholic beverages in the home. A change was made, and a cocktail hour, with beer and wine, was introduced, organized and supervised by a committee of the residents.

Conclusion

Each of these examples of applied quantitative research shows how a mix of expertise and careful gathering and management of complex data systems are helpful in testing the assumptions of common sense among presumed "experts." They also show how fairly elaborate data on particular social conditions among a program's clientele can reveal patterns not initially visible to the professionals themselves.

In addition, these examples illustrate both advantages and hazards of cooperation and close communication between academic researchers and program administrators. And even the negative results, which could have been more politically volatile had the research staff vigorously publicized selected findings in the local media, suggest the necessity for at least a degree of institutional independence in executing research on delivery of public programs.

PART II
Policy Analysis for Export to the Developing World

The craftspersons of policy analysis in the West, at least within traditional social science disciplines, have resisted exporting their products to the Third World. Having been burned all too often in the past by attempting to fit Western models and research priorities to unfamiliar settings, perhaps they are justified in this resistance.

Social scientists, however, with more fervent (or at least more obvious) ideological commitments have not hesitated to prescribe drastic revisions in the policy directions chosen by Third World countries and by Western regimes that would seek to aid or exploit them. Perhaps a dose of mundane, empirical, quantitative policy analysis, coupled with closer on-site observation, could help reduce the heat-to-light ratio in research on national development.

Chapter 4, coauthored with my colleague Üstün Ergüder of Boğaziçi University in Istanbul, examines specifically the relative fit to a Third World context of the simple systems model generally adopted by political scientists studying policy in the West. By and large, a positive report is delivered on the utility of the approach, so long as certain key cautions are observed.

Chapter 5 argues that the mix of analytic tools used by policy analysts must be adapted to the actual priorities pursued in the countries studied. Particularly, I suggest that our research tactics to date have been ill-fitted to the major thrust of development policy toward basic needs of the poor in the poorest countries.

Chapter 6 proposes an additional view or stance for enhancing the utility of policy research in some of the most poor parts of the world. The reader will quickly note that this chapter is not written in the customary manner of scholarly essays. It is, in many respects, a portion of a travelogue. It offers some very personal observations on aspects

of development in the Third World which are often not made explicit
in formal publications.

I include this chapter not only for its substantive recommendations
but also to make as clear as possible my own normative commitments
with regard to the development process. Policy analysis goes beyond
the rather tattered arguments for value-free inquiry. Policy analysis, at
its most useful, at its most intersubjective, and at its most objective,
reveals normative preferences and then arrays evidence to support hypotheses about the maximization of those preferences.

An additional reason for including this unorthodox essay is to convey
clearly the nature of the evidence upon which my recommendations are
based. There are many types of evidence (and many types of experiences
in gathering evidence) in the social sciences. The necessity to reveal
one's data-gathering techniques is, if anything, higher when those methods are more unconventional and founded on peculiar (perhaps non-
replicable) experiences of the investigator.

Based on observations made in Nepal, particularly with respect to
the development of domestic water systems, the argument in Chapter
6 is for adding a "bottom-up" approach to the other strategies of development research that are commonly pursued.

4

The Penetrability of Policy Systems in a Developing Context

With Üstün Ergüder

Is the policy systems paradigm commonly employed in the West useful as a guide to analysis in developing countries? This chapter addresses that question, primarily in reference to Turkey, but with a serious effort to extend the observations to other developing countries.

What are the general contours of the systems paradigm that has become most widely used to analyze the causes and consequences of public policies in Western welfare states? How exportable is that paradigm to less developed countries (LDCs)? What guidance does research conducted within that paradigm provide to persons committed to system change?

For all their more or less institutionalized self-criticism, ignoring certain fringe revolutionary elements, most of the Western democracies do not show a widespread desire to be something other than what they are. To be sure, progress is desired. Economic reverses stimulate anxiety. But there is no common agreement as to the worth of one or another definition of progress relative to present conditions. Especially in the period of retarded growth and economic stagnation that began in the mid-1970s, one cannot accuse analysts of Western societies of an excess of smug self-satisfaction. But one does not find among the carriers of ideology in the West a fundamental commitment to transforming the system radically. The "preservation/change ratio" is higher than in less developed countries.

Certainly the ratio is lower in Turkey than in the countries that have produced the bulk of empirical policy analysis. Turkish experts will argue over the extent of commitment to Kemalist ideology (i.e., that which traces its roots to the sayings and actions of Mustafa Kemal Atatürk). But few will deny that the commitment to modernization—a transformation of Turkey from what it *is* or has been to something it yet *is not*—is certainly widespread among the carriers of the republic's founding ideology.

This commitment to transforming the system is reflected in social research by a relatively higher degree of concern for the levers of change, identification of points for purposeful intervention, and relatively less concern, compared to Western empirical research, for the more reflective task of explanation. Clearly, rational intervention is helped by good explanatory theory. In order purposefully and permanently to change some circumstance it helps to know what causes that circumstance. We are not suggesting that the activist mode of scholarship is pursued in Turkey to the exclusion of good empirical-historical explanation, but the relative balance of concern for change versus preservation flows throughout research by Turks about Turkey.

In assessing the fit of an imported paradigm, therefore, it is reasonable to test not only the extent to which it leads one to ask interesting questions but also to the extent to which it suggests useful questions. Our test of the policy paradigm is based on three criteria: Are the questions suggested important to Turkey (and, by risky extension, to other less developed countries)? Are other important questions left out or devalued below their real importance in the Turkish context? Does the strategy of inquiry lead one to distinguish between controllable and uncontrollable forces?

Our conclusion is that the policy systems paradigm passes these tests. The questions suggested are important. No major categories of important concerns seem to be excluded. And the tentative answers seem helpful in identifying controllable, or changeable, elements in the task of system transformation.

The systems paradigm has led Western research to focus on several questions. A key one asks, To what extent is variance in policy outputs the result of variance in political and institutional circumstances? Put in practical terms, can one expect a change of leadership, party, or even constitutional rules to affect the mix of policies a country produces? Is sufficient control available to be exercised over the policy-making apparatuses that such political changes will have an effect on policies?

The political scientists interested in comparative policy analysis have been concerned about this family of questions. In the present context, that translates into the overall question, Are political differences more or less consequential for policy in LDCs, compared to their seemingly equivocal importance in more affluent countries?

The systems paradigm poses another link, this one between policy instruments and social conditions. Policy evaluators ask, To what extent does variance in policy actually applied to social conditions have intended effects on those conditions? This is the question, of course, which is central to the modes of analysis discussed in the first three chapters in this book. Do comparable policy instruments, conscientiously applied, have more or less effect in LDCs than elsewhere? If policies can be "delivered," is there more or less hope for their making a difference in LDCs? Or are the rigidities of those countries such as to put them beyond the grasp of effective treatment by known policy instruments?

Policies of known effectiveness elsewhere may be politically blocked from enactment in specific settings. For example, certain birth control policies may not be acceptable in particular religious climates. Likewise, policies whose worth was proven elsewhere may not work in specific settings. Male medical practitioners, proven effective in some settings, may not receive cooperation where certain cultural norms prevent particular types of male-female contact. Between these two sets of concerns, the politics → policy and the policy → society links, lies another potentially weak link posed by the systems paradigm. This is the administrative, or implementation, link. Is the likelihood of faithful implementation of policy makers' directives higher or lower in LDCs, compared to more affluent countries?

Put together, these concerns, posed by the policy systems model, lead one to investigate the policy process pretty much in terms of the following schematic:

Politics → Policy → Implementation → Social Targets

To highlight the concern for a strategy of explanation that helps set priorities for intervention, we employ the concept of *penetrability*. At the most general level, this concept fits the question, for each sector of the policy process, How penetrable is that sector by causal factors that lie within the range of purposeful change?[1] Put otherwise, it seeks to array the panoply of determinants according to their relative susceptibility to deliberate intervention (Hofferbert and Sande, 1976).

In this regard, this chapter elaborates and explores three hypotheses. Specifically, in comparison to Western industrial polities, policy systems in LDCs are more penetrable by implemented political change; social conditions in LDCs are more penetrable by policy; and administrative-bureaucratic structures of LDCs are less penetrable by policy directives.

To aid understanding of the constraints and opportunities within the Turkish context, and to alert one to areas of potential misfit of an alien analytical paradigm, it will be helpful to have a bit of general background on the development of the public sector in Turkey.

The Ottoman Turkish Bureaucratic Tradition

A comparison of western European and Ottoman-Turkish social and political historical sequences is the reference point needed to highlight the most relevant differences. One of the distinctive characteristics of western European development is the autonomy of state and society during different historical periods. In other words, western European society may in general be characterized by the existence of a civil society quite distinct from the state. In the West, social and political structures have not been coterminous and inseparable. During the Middle Ages, relationships between feudal lords and the king were based on relatively clear definitions of reciprocal rights and duties. The emergence of trade in western Europe and the demise of feudalism witnessed the rise of mercantilism and royal absolutism. The general result was that the decentralized juridical character of feudalism was not compatible with the newly emerging marketplace and all the autonomous relations associated with the market. The order of the day was a strong authority at the center, which could protect frontiers, improve communications, administer a common unit of exchange, and see to it that the same legal principles would apply within given borders. Royal absolutism was a response to social and economic need arising from an autonomously functioning marketplace and the social relations associated and intermeshed with it. The state and its bureaucracy provided essential services for more efficient functioning of the market.

The rise of political liberalism may be seen as an attempt by social forces organized around the market (bourgeoisie) to limit power of the central authority, that is, the society's effort to control the instruments of the state, as a definable specialized entity. Central authority, strengthened and organized but unchecked, may be detrimental to the autonomous functioning of the marketplace it is supposed to enhance. In fact, one could say that political liberalism and the associated concept of limited government were attempts to keep the state and its bureaucracy in the service of an autonomously functioning, market-based civil society. The bureaucracy was a service to the marketplace.

The rise of the welfare state in western Europe, with the corresponding extension of the role of the state in economic affairs, coincided with further democratization. The transformation and expansion of the bureaucracy did not fundamentally alter its role in service to the civil society. The growing importance of masses, and especially working classes, in politics and economic life, along with increased perception of imperfections in the market working against those groups, led to a redefinition, via ideologies, of the role of the state in economic affairs. The state, through regulatory, distributive, and redistributive policies and services, could intervene in the market to protect those groups suffering from the imperfections of the market (Flora and Heidenheimer, 1981a). An important point to remember is that the rise of the welfare state involves extending the concept of *state in the service of society* so dominant in western Europe. The regulatory and control-oriented policies developed in and defining the welfare state, as well as the practices to implement policy, were shaped and influenced by this predominant service tradition.

The Ottoman-Turkish tradition stands in contrast to the western European experience. Turkey inherited and sustained a large, ancient bureaucracy, predating the emergence of liberal economic or political practices. The chief function of that bureaucracy has not been social service but social control.

The emphasis on the control function of the Turkish bureaucracy is a consequence of the special relationship that the state and society in the Ottoman Empire had vis-à-vis each other. That relationship was not premised on mutual autonomy. Rather, it was symbolized by a patrimonialism through which the state dominated and controlled the society, especially in tax collection and conscription. True to its patrimonial role, the center (state) would provide welfare (*hisba*) and justice in return for loyalty (Mardin, 1969). In the words of a prominent Turkish social scientist: "The Ottoman Empire lacked those intermediate structures which both Machiavelli and Montesquieu regarded as constituting the

difference between Eastern despotism and Western feudalism. It lacked
that basic structural component that Hegel termed 'civil society', a part
of the society that could operate independently of central government
and was based on property rights'' (Mardin, 1969). Thus one of the
most important characteristics of the Ottoman Empire was that, in the
absence of horizontal integration through the market, the sate played a
central role in providing vertical integration.

A set of policies was necessary for the state to hold the society together
in view of the lack of horizontal integration. A system of rewards (*hisba*
and justice) and sanctions, coupled with central bureaucracy hierarchi-
cally organized, was an integral part of this tradition. The central bureaucracy, through a very complex system of patronage, would work
through local notables, acting as agents of the central government. The
center was mainly interested in extracting soldiers (conscripts) and taxes
for the successful pursuit of *gaza* (conquest and plunder), an important
policy for creating economic surplus for the empire. Loyalty of the local
notables as well as of the peasantry was extremely important for the
preservation of the empire. The loyalty of the local notables was secured
through granting usufruct on land owned by the state or by providing
economic and social privileges. Distribution of *hisba* and justice, and
thus protection of the peasant against the local notables, was an important objective of the state to sustain the allegiance of the peasantry
(Mardin, 1969, 1971, 1973; Inalçik, 1964).

The evidence suggests that the bureaucracy in the Ottoman Empire
existed well before the rise of the market. It served as the Ottoman
center's essential instrument for control of the periphery and for integration of the empire via the center in the absence of horizontal market
linkages. Surely the concept of welfare as state policy existed in the
empire long before its emergence in the western European context.
Welfare generally meant a collection of policies granted by the state for
the purpose of controlling a heterogeneous empire and social periphery.
Welfare in the western European context, on the other hand, stood for
a group of policies extracted by social forces from the state in response
to the imperfections of the market. Our contention here is that policies
in the Ottoman Empire, which might be substantively analogous to
Western examples, were largely conditioned by and executed within a
control rather than a service paradigm.

It is safe to assume that this peculiar state and bureaucratic tradition
had a continuing influence in the Turkish republic after the Kemalist

revolution of the 1920s. One of the most important characteristics of the Atatürk revolution in Turkey was its conservatism: it was a revolution from the top, a political rather than a social revolution. The leadership cadre was a military-bureaucratic intelligentsia trained in the course of the earlier reform and Westernization attempts by the Ottomans, which had been aimed at arresting the decline of the empire through reform of the military and civilian bureaucratic apparatuses (Rustow, 1968; Mardin, 1969; Sunar, 1974).

It is interesting to trace the impact of the Ottoman bureaucratic heritage on republican policies. Control of a far-flung Anatolian periphery was still a nagging concern for the Kemalist elite. Kemalism, however, was also strongly committed to modernizing the society, both socially and economically. This meant that the state would now take a more active role in economic life, especially in infrastructural investments, because of the lack of private entrepreneurial personnel and capital (Ahmad, 1981; Boratav, 1981). Thus in the 1930s *étatism* (statism) was declared as a general economic policy, through which the state would directly engage in production as well as play a leadership role in providing incentives to help develop an indigenous private enterprise. Over 40 percent of industrial production in Turkey in the 1980s was still the responsibility of state economic enterprises, heavily subsidized by general revenues.

Étatism, in this sense, was hardly a challenge to the state-bureaucratic tradition inherited from the Ottomans. But to control was added a novel state function: production. The state and its bureaucracy would assume guardianship of economic and social modernization. It is no wonder that the state in Turkey is known as the Father State (*devlet baba*), and, during times of crisis, saving the state is equated with saving the society itself.

Our question here is, Do the key differences in bureaucratic traditions and practices render utterly inapplicable to Turkey (and other developing countries with comparable distinguishing features) the main strategic elements of the policy analysis paradigm as produced in the West?

The Systems Paradigm of Comparative Policy Analysis

At the macrohistorical level, the most elegant formulation of the paradigm most often used to explain the causes of policy variance is probably to be found in Peter Flora and Jens Alber's examination of the determinants of welfare state policies in Europe (1981). The roots go back at least to studies of American state politics in the mid-1960s (Dawson and Robinson, 1963. For reviews, see Hofferbert, 1972; Castles, 1982b; Hancock, 1982; Hofferbert and Schäfer, 1982). Without attempting a comprehensive review here, we wish merely to point out the uncommon commonality that characterizes the general field of inquiry. The key question asked in the comparative policy output literature is, What causes variation over time or across jurisdictions in the measurable outputs of the policy process? The determinants investigated customarily are divided into socioeconomic forces and political conditions. From an early focus on rather static models, employing cross-sectional correlations, the field has moved to an admirable level of quantitatively sophisticated, historically informed inquiry. One salutary result of the move from exclusively cross-sectional correlation and regression analysis to much more elegant (if technically less imposing) historically sensitive research has been an abandonment of unduly simplistic formulations of key questions.

The central question for many years was, Which is more important, economics or politics? Enough partial correlations between indicators of socioeconomic development, party competition, and public expenditures were produced to clog the lines of any reasonable attempt at synthesis. We would observe, editorially, that a reading beyond the few root articles written in the mid-1960s ought to put to rest, once and for all, this intrusive simplification (Mazmanian and Sabatier, 1980s; Flora and Alber, 1981; Schmidt, 1982; Castles, 1982b). As was already demonstrated by many pieces in the late 1960s and early 1970s, the question is not the relative importance of politics versus economics but rather the dynamics of their interaction as determinants within a policy system (e.g., Cnudde and McCrone, 1969; Walker, 1969; Sharkansky and Hofferbert, 1969; Grumm, 1973; Lewis-Beck, 1977; Flora and Heidenheimer, 1981a; Hofferbert, 1981).

Having asserted, however, that the juxtaposition of politics and economics tilted toward the naive, we are nonetheless not claiming that the policy systems that have been investigated in the West are laid wide open to short-term manipulation by the whiffs and puffs of political change.

From the standpoint of our concern with "penetrability," the driving force of most of this research was the early failure of many careful investigators to find policy consequences of political variation. Regardless of what voters or constitution writers might have done, the results of their efforts seemed only dimly reflected in the products of governmental deliberation, once the effects of relatively unmanageable socioeconomic forces were controlled (Cutright, 1965; Wilensky, 1975). In our terms, that would be an assertion that the decision apparatuses of governments were relatively impenetrable by politics.

Much of the inability to detect the role of politics in policy, holding constant major economic and social conditions, was a function of the cross-sectional mode of analysis. Flora and his colleagues are able to show the effect of political change on various aspects of welfare state policy when these political conditions are measured at the time of major policy innovations. Incrementalism and the accretion of confounding forces fog such political consequentiality when measured several decades after the fact (Flora and Heidenheimer, 1981a; Flora and Alber, 1981; Alber, 1981; Kuhnle, 1981).

The evolution of greater precision in estimating the joint and independent effects of political and socioeconomic factors in no way detracts from the vitality of the concepts and the utility of investigating them as determinants of policy variance. That is, this component of the paradigm has worked well, at least in the Western context. If one wants to know why policies vary, either over time or across jurisdictions, it is a good idea to try to measure the relationship of those policies to major dimensions of socioeconomic and political variance.

To the extent that political forces are independently relevant, we speak of the "political penetrability" of the policy system. The extent of political penetrability of the policy system is the extent to which political change leads to distinct policy changes. Will a military coup change policies in a predictable fashion? Will a return from military to popular rule have a predictable effect in the opposite direction?

The results of the most elegant quantitative historical work in the West suggest that the sorting out of relevant political consequences in the growth of the welfare state, though manageable, is a far from simple or straightforward task (Flora and Heidenheimer, 1981a). Below we discuss the grounds for our acceptance of the initial hypothesis that political penetrability is higher in LDCs than in the more affluent countries, which have served generally as the sites for comparative studies of policy outputs.

Although the political science community is relatively familiar with and agreed upon strategies for the comparative analysis of policy *causes*, research on policy *consequences* is considerably less secure on its agenda of intellectual priorities. Policy evaluation, as discussed in Part I, grew rapidly as a money-making industry among substantive experts (e.g., education, health, and transportation). But social scientists in general, and political scientists in particular, have been insecure and uncertain as to their competitive advantage in that business. Much of this hesitancy is visible in the pages of new policy journals that have emerged in recent years (e.g., the *Policy Studies Journal,* its offspring, the *Policy Studies Review,* and the *Journal of Public Policy).* Those who have ventured into the fray of evaluation research find themselves dealing with a wild and bizarre range of dependent variables: workers' attitudes (Hedlund and Nachmias, 1980), dietary behavior of the elderly (Cingranelli et al., 1981), income distribution (McCrone and Hardy, 1978), and others. As a discipline, political science has not decided where it belongs in such a diverse range of inquiry, especially when the things needing measurement are so uncommon to the professional ken of the practitioners.[2]

A brief overview of the form of evaluation research (research on the consequences of policy) reveals, however, a remarkable structural similarity to the paradigmatic concerns of the output (or policy causes) work with which political scientists have become familiar over the past several years. The dependent variable of evaluation research is the social condition or target of policy outputs, either at the individual or at the structural level. Policies are usually designed to do something to or for people. Measurement of the extent to which the policy actually does something to or for the social target is what evaluation research is all about.

To assess the impact of policy on a social condition, it is necessary to control for factors other than policy which may have brought about that condition. In this sense, the social condition of evaluation research is analogous to the "output" in comparative policy research. The policy of evaluation research is analogous to political conditions in comparative policy research. That is, the seemingly controllable aspect of the output model, the leverage point, is the political antecedent of policy (Schmidt, 1982). Similarly, the policy is the controllable antecedent or the leverage point of social conditions. In the latter case, one must control for prior individual or collective socioeconomic conditions (i.e., the causes that are less manipulable and yet compete for explanatory force with policy). In the former case, similarly, it is necessary to control for the socioeconomic conditions that are antecedent to or compete as explanatory forces with politics as causes of policy itself.

Thus in their effort to assess the impact of the Comprehensive Employment and Training Act on workers' attitudes, Ronald Hedlund and Nachmias Chaua (1980) had to control for personal socioeconomic traits, prior work experience, and other factors. To test the effect of participation in a federally funded hot lunch program for the elderly, David Cingranelli and his colleagues (1981) had to control for individual socioeconomic status, personal values, and so on. To assess the impact of civil rights and antipoverty legislation on the black-white income ratio, D. McCrone and R. Hardy (1978) had to control for regional traits, unemployment rates, and economic growth.

The paradigm of policy evaluation is virtually the same as for output research. It is just that it has moved over one box in the systems diagram. The simplified model of output research is illustrated in Figure 4.1. The simplified model of evaluation research is illustrated in Figure 4.2.

When output researchers bother to present a systems diagram, they always include a "feedback" arrow from their dependent variable (policy output) back to the socioeconomic conditions box. Clearly, evaluation research constitutes the substance of that feedback arrow. Policy analysts are beginning to realize that these two domains of research fit together into a single, dynamic policy process model (Hofferbert and Schäfer, 1982).

To the extent that policies can have an impact on their target that is

Figure 4.1 The Simplified Policy Evaluation Model

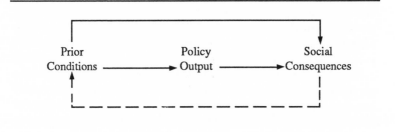

Figure 4.2   The Simplified Policy Output Model

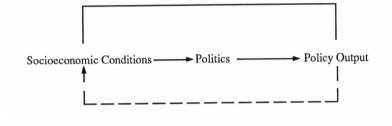

in the expected (i.e., hoped-for) direction, independent of the effect of prepolicy circumstances, we refer to policies having "social penetrability." Unfortunately, as the discussion of the Great Society policies in Chapter 1 suggested, the record of the capacity of Western governments to intervene beneficially is more limited than might be desired by compassionate advocates of innovative programs. The penetrability of complex societies by policy seems about as limited as the political penetrability of their decision structures (Hofferbert, 1982). This lack of clear policy effectiveness has stimulated a range of inquiry into the impediments to beneficial intervention. Increasing attention is being given, in particular, to the domain of policy implementation, the linkage between output and impact.

The same degree of paradigmatic regularity found in output and impact research does not yet exist in the field of implementation studies. The necessity for looking to the implementation process for explanations of the apparent ineffectiveness of policies has been amply demonstrated in several case studies, the most widely cited of which is that by Jeffrey Pressman and Aaron Wildavsky (1979). The study of policy implementation can be said to be at the preparadigm stage. What fits into it is less clear than what it fits into.

The field is fairly clearly identified: the study of those conditions, organizational settings, and human behaviors that affect the translation of policy pronouncements into public goods, services, and regulations. There is hardly yet an agreed priority for control variables, causal sequences, or particular hypotheses. Recent work at the preoperational stage, however, suggests that some such order may be emerging.

Paul Sabatier and Daniel Mazmanian have offered a conceptual framework which appears to hold high promise, as evidenced by initial efforts at application (1980b). Specifically, they identify several potentially generalizable subsets of three major categories of factors which are likely to affect the achievement of statutory objectives: the tractability of the problem(s) addressed by a statute; the ability of the statute to structure favorably the implementation process; and the net effect of a variety of political variables on the balance of support for statutory objectives.

One could argue that their classification spills over from implementation characteristics to the range of components customarily examined in evaluation research. Within the subsets of factors included in the three major categories, however, one finds components that are purely implementational and of apparent generalizability across policies and contexts. For example, under the extent to which a statute coherently structures the implementation process, Sabatier and Mazmanian direct attention to such elements as the extent of hierarchical integration within and among implementing institutions; the extent to which decision rules of implementing agencies are supportive of statutory objectives; the assignment of programs to implementing agencies and officials committed to statutory objectives; and the extent to which opportunities for participation by actors external to the implementing agencies are biased toward supporters of statutory objectives.

In essence, these guidelines and the general message of implementation studies is that one should not mistake inadequate implementation for ill-designed policies. In the face of evidence indicating poor fit between the impact and the goal of policies, it has been too often the case that the analyst challenges the theory upon which the policy is based rather than investigating if it was ever even adequately attempted, the existence of statutory exhortation to the contrary notwithstanding (Palumbo and Sharp, 1980).

We denote as "administrative penetrability" the extent to which a statute or other policy output is likely to be faithfully executed. Administrative penetrability does not measure the extent to which a policy "works" (that is social penetrability), but rather the extent to which it is given a fair shot.

Fit of the Paradigm in an LDC

Even given the relative imbalance in analytical development between output and impact research compared to implementation studies, it is clear that they fit together into a nice dynamic model, the key elements of which are portrayed in Figure 4.3. (Compound paths should be considered when reasonable.) It has worked in the West, as evidenced by interesting and useful research results (Hofferbert and Schäfer, 1982).

Will it fit in a less developed country? There are reasons to warrant doubt. What is known about the link between socioeconomic factors and politics suggests the unlikelihood of liberal political institutions below a particular level of industrialization, affluence, and national market integration (Cutright, 1963; Sunar, 1981). The politics that do seem to affect policy in the West are most often dramatically different, in stability, bargaining capacity, and other attributes, from their analogues in LDCs (Sunar, 1981; O'Donnell, 1973; Linz, 1978). The temporal sequence, discussed earlier in this chapter, of market development (economic liberalism), political liberalization, and emergence of the welfare state in the West is out of synchronization in most LDCs.

In other words, it is tempting to retreat to an ideographic mode and assert the uniqueness of the policy process in each less developed context. In the absence of a more attractive paradigm, which would drive rigorous, systematic empirical research by scholars in those contexts, such an assertion of paradigmatic irrelevance can be used as a com-

Figure 4.3   A Dynamic Policy Systems Model

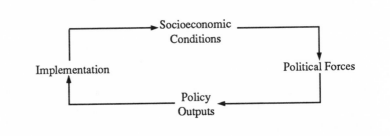

fortable excuse for avoiding the drudgery and frustration of concept measurement, data-grubbing, and technically sophisticated analysis.

In the absence of a demonstrably better set of guidelines, however, we are prepared to argue for the fit of the policy systems paradigm, even in a context as ostensibly different from Western welfare states as Turkey. To argue for the application of a set of categories, and even specific hypotheses, to a context different from that in which they were first developed does *not* require that we expect the coefficients of relationship to be the same, or even necessarily in the same direction, as in the original setting. The applicability of the paradigm, again, rests on its capacity to suggest and include the right sets of questions and to produce useful results.

Our own very preliminary research, as well as fairly extensive review of other existing studies, suggests that, while adopting the broad guidelines of the policy systems paradigm, we should also offer the following amending hypotheses, in line with our concept of penetrability:

The political penetrability of policy-making processes is inverse to the level of socioeconomic development. In comparative work across LDCs or time-series analysis intranationally, one should anticipate relatively strong correlation between variance in policy outputs and political conditions in those LDCs. A growing body of research in Turkey, for example, indicates that political, compared to socioeconomic, conditions are relatively more consequential as one goes down the development scale (ignoring for the present the bedeviling problem of multidimensionality and measurement on that scale) (see Ergüder, 1980b).

Because of greater social penetrability, once implemented, programs are more likely to attain their specific goals in a developing country. This is in contrast to the results of much evaluation research in the West, which frequently finds that programs have minimal direct, short-term positive impact. Penetrability by comparable policies is hypothesized to be inverse to the context's level of development.

Administrative penetrability is positively related to a country's level of development. Bureaucratic history, recruitment patterns, values, and incentive structures in LDCs reward control more than service and tend to block feedback channels, thus being less attuned to innovation than their Western counterparts.

One reason for the relatively greater political penetrability of policy in an LDC, controlling for socioeconomic context, is the simple likelihood that, if the particular country is making even an honest attempt at democratization, the raw political variance and discontinuity are greater than found in most Western countries (at least since World War II).

Turkey has had its ups and downs, but it still qualifies as one of the few demonstrable efforts at pluralistic democracy within the set of middle-income countries.[3] Since initiation of competitive politics in the late 1940s, political control has run the gamut from tight two-party competition to multiparty coalitions to three different military interventions. By the mid-1980s, political parties were allowed once again to operate on a fairly open basis, having been banned during the preceding period of military governance (1980–83). For whatever else that record may indicate, it surely indicates variance. And it is more variance than found in either stable authoritarian or stable democratic regimes.

Time series of different areas of public policy in Turkey indicate changes coincident with major parliamentary and regime adjustments. Research by one of the present authors, for example, clearly shows the coincidence of agricultural price support changes and competitive elections (Ergüder, 1980b). Likewise, although not yet tested with the same degree of precision, preliminary evidence suggests similar political correlates with other areas of public policy. The research base in Turkey is scant, compared to Western analyses, but to the extent that it exists, it supports the political penetrability hypothesis.

We should not rest the explanation, however, wholly on the statistical function resulting from broader political variance. Ideology cannot be ignored. In their current constitutional incarnations, most Western regimes are older than their less developed neighbors. New nations need a founding ideology or myth, usually attached to certain heroic figures. Washington, Lenin, Ho Chi Minh, Gandhi, and Atatürk all have been called from the grave to legitimize political change. To the extent that the ideology attached to their persons and the movements they are claimed to have inspired, if not founded, espouses radical social change, contemporary decision makers buy space for policy experimentation. Perhaps ironically, the greater the distance between what is and what is espoused, the greater the potential breadth of the policy agenda. And the greater the breadth of the agenda, the more likely that policy will vary as a measurable function of political change. Instability may be uncomfortable for the natives, but it enriches the research potential for the policy analyst.

Political practices are tenacious but probably a good deal more variant than economic structures, ethnic or religious identity, or even patterns of popular values. In that sense, governments, parties, and even constitutions can be changed more easily than those factors constituting the socioeconomic environment in most policy output research. If politics matters more for policy in LDCs, then we may anticipate a greater macro capacity for manipulating policies indirectly through political means in LDCs than in more modern political economies or welfare states.

Will it matter if policies are changed? If they are likely to be ineffective in bringing about their intended social objective, the apparent capacity for political intervention is but a chimera.

Politics are more volatile in the LDCs than in the West. And the difference in volatility for politics, between LDCs and the West, is probably greater than the variance in rates of socioeconomic change. But the latter also is more variant in many of the less developed countries, especially those in the middle range. The incremental, continuous pattern of socioeconomic evolution found above a certain level of industrialization and affluence provides a contextual constraint that is institutionalized in the policy process, thus limiting the vulnerability or amenability of social conditions to significant impact from deliberate adjustments or innovations in policy. The stability of society is surely greater than are political practices in LDCs, if such implicit scales are comparable at all. But social change, too, in areas of high policy relevance, moves there at a rate that is uncommon in the West.

Important social conditions change in the middle-income countries at a comparatively rapid rate. Economic structural conditions (e.g.., productive sectoral shares), economic climates (e.g., GNP growth or inflation rates), and basic life circumstances (e.g., life expectancy, infant mortality) are all relatively more susceptible to the forces of change as one moves down the scale of economic development (ignoring, in the present context, whether that pace of change may be flatter among the very poorest countries).

Our proposal is that such volatility increases the vulnerability or receptivity of a society to effective intervention by policy instruments.

Thus our second major hypothesis is that LDCs are more socially penetrable than their industrialized or postindustrialized neighbors.

At first, this idea seems to fly in the face of common observations on the seeming intractability of problems in many LDCs. One problem substitutes for another. Rural overpopulation and economic stagnation are "cured" by massive migration to underserviced cities, yielding sprawling squatter settlements, congestion, health hazards, and occasional violence (Ergüder, 1980b). Whether there are only two steps backward for every three forward is often hard to divine. A massive irrigation project, for example, promised to revolutionize agricultural production in the Çukorova Valley in Turkey (in the south coastal region around Adana). It did that, but the irrigated areas were improperly drained, providing breeding grounds for anopholese mosquitoes and a tragic rise in the incidence of malaria (Yumer, 1980).

Costly by-products of well-intentioned policies are not a monopoly of underdeveloped countries, as the history of urban renewal and transportation policies in the West can attest (Downs, 1974). There are bright sides, however, that may be relatively brighter in the LDCs. That is, formally comparable policies may be expected, if delivered, to produce a relatively higher cost-effectiveness ratio in the LDC context than in the West.

This expectation is principally an extension of a pattern discernible in Western evaluation research. Strong clues in much of that research suggest that the cost-effectiveness of programs is dramatically variant as a function of the needs of target groups (Hofferbert, 1982). Participants in Milwaukee's Comprehensive Employment and Training program generally had poorer attitudes toward work after their program experience than before, but the participants with a history of welfare dependency and unemployment did not (Hedlund and Nachmias, 1980). The U.S. poverty and civil rights programs of the mid-1960s had only modest detectable impact on black-white income ratios nationally, but there was a dramatic effect in the South, where the initial condition was most stark (McCrone and Hardy, 1978). On the average, participants in the federally sponsored hot lunch programs for the elderly showed no significant dietary differences from nonparticipants, but there were noticeable benefits among the very poorest elderly who lived alone (Cingranelli et al., 1981). Most participants in the New Jersey income guarantee became less involved in the labor force but not the male blacks, who were initially the worst off (Rees, 1974).

These and other studies finding minimal mean effect of social service policies in the United States also show high impact at the high-need end of the continuum of recipients, suggesting a diminishing curve of cost-effectiveness as one moves away from the most needy targets (Hofferbert, 1982). By extension, one could speculate that comparable programs would be likely to yield greater cost-effectiveness in a less developed country, where most indicators of social need are patently higher. Thus a massive, multifaceted adult literacy program was initiated at the time of Atatürk's substitution of the Roman alphabet for the old Arabic form of Turkish script. Illiteracy was cut from above 90 percent in the late 1920s to its present 30 to 35 percent. The next 10 percent reduction will be more difficult, however, than the last, if measured by unit costs. But still it will be far less difficult and expensive than a comparably structured and funded effort would be in the United States, where the reduction would have to focus on the last 1 to 2 percent of the population who are illiterate.

Improvement of public health is a greater challenge when many of the major historical causes of mortality and morbidity have been brought within the reach of modern medicine's capacities. But when half of the deaths in a country are children under five years of age (as recent statistics indicate is the case in Turkey), the question is not *what* service to deliver, but *how* to deliver it. If the shots can be administered, deaths by measles, currently one of the three leading causes of child deaths in Turkey, will practically stop. Tuberculosis was a major killer in Turkey until very recent years. It has been dramatically reduced, in large part through publicly designed and administered programs, using techniques known and proven elsewhere.

Current projections warrant optimism in reducing population growth from 2.5 percent to approximately 2.0 percent. Getting it down from 2.0 percent to 1.5 percent, not to mention zero growth, will be vastly more difficult.

In other words, the attack on many social pathologies in LDCs does not confront a problem of policy theory. The society, as a function of absolute need level, is penetrable by known policy instruments. Scattered evidence from evaluation research, executed almost exclusively by substantive specialists rather than by social scientists in Turkey, bears out this assertion. Controlling for prepolicy conditions, research is available to confirm the beneficial effects of delivered policies. The paradigm used by evaluation research fits as well as the policy output component.

The problem, from the standpoints of both analysis and social intervention, is not what to do but how to do it. That is, the priority is not on what policies can penetrate the society but what will make the structure of implementation more penetrable by policy.

Our third major hypothesis suggests that LDCs are less administratively penetrable than their industrialized or postindustrialized counterparts. In other words, we expect policy outputs in LDCs to run into administrative barriers or at least to be reshaped or changed substantially at the implementation stage, out of proportion to Western experience. What administrative barriers policies encounter or how they are reshaped or changed is, we assert, a function of endogenous social, cultural, and historical conditions. In their comparative study of Korean and Turkish civil services, for example, Martin Heper, Chong Lim Kim, and Seong-Tong Pai conclude that ''The historical bureaucratic tradition, rather than variations in regime types, may offer better explanations of the behaviors of the public service in some developing countries, especially where there exists a firmly established tradition of the civil service.'' (1980, p. 153).

We readily admit that the causes of administrative impenetrability are likely to vary from one LDC to another. For example, in the 1960s Fred Riggs attracted attention to the point that exaggerated efforts to develop merit-oriented bureaucracies, which would in turn act as agents of modernization, might lead to immobile and politically unresponsive civil services in LDCs (1966). It is fair to expect that in an LDC where resources have been liberally allocated to develop bureaucratic institutions, and where political institutions are less developed, administrative responsiveness to policy decisions made elsewhere will be low. It is strongly urged here, however, that the emphasis on meritocracy, the desire to rationalize policy choice, and the conceptualization of the state as the major agent of modernization may not be the only variables to explain the lack of administrative penetrability in LDCs. The Turkish experience suggests that historical bureaucratic tradition and the role of Ottoman and Turkish bureaucracy (not to mention the likely lineage back to Byzantine practices) in a distinctively different social and political history are equally, if not more, important explanatory elements.

Conclusion: Bases for Generalization?

The set of less developed countries, though widely variant in their historical and institutional evolution, share in common an exemption from the Western sequence. Their bureaucracies have been there since long before the emergence of the market, if the market has yet emerged. Bureaucracies did not, therefore, emerge as a corrective of the market, spurred by political liberalization, any more than the state earlier emerged as an aid to the market.

The concept of control of the bureaucracy by more or less popularly invested political institutions (such as congressional oversight) is far less visible in LDCs than in the West. More common in the former is a pattern that, in some important respects, reverses the flow of control. Bureaucracies that preceded the rise of the civil society are more likely to assume the role of guardian than of servant.

The state administrative apparatus stands as a rare channel for upward social mobility, a potential that was historically and is currently lacking in the private sectors. Meritocratic recruitment and advancement rules (whether historically inherited, as in the Ottoman-Turkish tradition, or installed during colonial rule or in the immediate postcolonial period) reinforce a sense of insularity within the bureaucracy. Such rules, as Riggs predicted, rather than ensuring an ethos of service for "clients," led to defensiveness vis-à-vis political controls from the top and a disdain for the putative clients of public agencies.

The guardianship function is reinforced rather than muted by a frequent pattern of uneasy balance or competition between multiple organizations of control within the remnants of former empires (e.g., Turkey) or postcolonial polities (e.g., Egypt). The chief competitor is usually the military, sometimes compounded by a bureaucratized single-party hierarchy. One or the other (in Turkey's case, the army) carries a constitutional protectionist idology, stemming form the heroic record as a revolutionary elite. Certainly such describes the place of the Turkish military as the self-proclaimed defender of pure Kemalism and protector of the Atatürk revolution.

Postrevolutionary or postcolonial military bureaucracies, resistant to popularly endowed political instruments, either elective officials or party functionaries, are often suspicious of the conformity of the state bureaucracy to revolutionary ideals, especially when the bureaucracy is one of the few social organs to have survived form before and through the revolutionary period. Evidence of political infiltration is seen by the state bureaucracy as unethical and as a threat to professional standards (and the fruits of mobility). It is similarly viewed by the military as counterrevolutionary. State bureaucrats, looking over their shoulders, as it were, are sensitive to their responsibility for preventing popular behaviors that might be viewed by the revolutionary guardians (either military or party) as evidence of deviation from the heroic mission. The net result, without warranting a union between competing hierarchies, is an ideology of control, a disincentive for responsiveness to claims from the bottom up, and a systematic diffusion of responsibility.

In those rare cases when not one but a plurality of popularly endowed organizations, approximating political parties, can secure some degree of effective control over the established bureaucracy(ies), opportunities for programmatic innovation aimed toward service rather than control become possible. Such cases are not numerous, nor have they been adequately documented by systematic inquiry.

The suggestion, therefore, is that appropriate sites for concentrated policy analysis in the developing world may well be those few areas where a degree of pluralistic political experience has been gained (e.g., Costa Rica, India, and Turkey). More specifically, within those settings a focus is needed on policy innovations that have worked, that is, the administrative structures have been penetrated by novel policies of a distinctly service nature.

The most interesting period in Turkish political history, for example, in which to test administrative penetrability, is probably the period between 1950 and the present, when a genuine attempt was made to experiment with a multiparty democracy, despite periodic disruptions. Political parties emerged and had notable success in organizing peripheral elements around the marketplace (Ergüder and Hofferbert, 1984). They have challenged the role of the bureaucracy, so much shaped by and long committed to the control paradigm.

The net effect of these changes is difficult to gauge, but perusal of relevant studies of policy implementation suggest that the record, in recent years, is not one of total administrative impenetrability. Some important policy innovations in diverse areas (e.g., irrigation, health service delivery, and adult literacy) have been implemented and obtained notable success (Atav, 1984). An effect-success ratio would be hard to construct. But the direction for theoretically interesting and socially useful research is clear: we should search for the levers and mechanisms of implementation which characterize these positive, deviant cases. In planning such inquiry, we anticipate beneficial guidance from recent Western theoretical progress on implementation (e.g., Sabatier and Mazmanian, 1980).

To recapitulate, we see LDCs as relatively politically penetrable, that is, decision-making systems are less constrained by socioeconomic resources than in the West and more open to politically determined innovations. Likewise, as a function of more stark conditions of need and socioeconomic volatility, we see the social penetrability of LDCs as higher, that is, amenable to treatment by services with a higher likelihood of marginal sucess, once delivered.

The bottleneck is in the delivery process, the administrative impenetrability of LDCs. The premature evolution of large central bureaucracies in LDCs (if Turkey's experience is indicative) yields a control rather than a service orientation, relative to the Western situation. Scholars seeking ways around this bottleneck, once the hypothesis that it is there is confirmed, are well-advised to explore cases of deviation, that is, instances of successful implementation. Better theory will be built as a result of that exploration.

Upon reflection, one can expect a pessimistic response to the admonition, Find successful policies and see how they were delivered. How does one systematically find successful policies? In the absence of a solid base of evaluation research, how can one be sure what constitutes a successful policy and then distinguish it from what is merely, in classic spurious form, the result of social changes exogenous or causally antecedent to the policy? And what are the chances for conducting widespread evaluation in a time frame that has a scintilla of utility under rapidly changing political circumstances?

Fortunately and surprisingly, the field of evaluation research is not barren in Turkey or in other LDCs (e.g., Freeman et al., 1979). Initial

searches reveal a reasonably rich storehouse of narrowly focused, substantively specialized, but scientifically respectable evaluation studies.
They have not, as a matter of course, fallen within the purview of
political scientists. In fact, many are limited in physical availability,
with the few known copies languishing on dusty shelves in middle-level
ministerial offices. UNESCO, ILO, WHO, and similar organizations
have often been the progenitors of such research. Indigenous studies
have also come from the (often fitful) efforts at national economic
planning. And such studies, though physically and substantively scattered, are frequently known within narrow circles of subject area experts.

When we have consulted those experts about problems in their re-
spective areas (e.g., health care delivery, literacy programs, agricultural
extension), their diagnoses do not reflect lack of enthusiasm or evidence
for potential benefit from known modes of "treatment." Their common
frustration, often bordering on what political scientists would consider
naive, is directed toward the bureaucracy.

If indeed the barriers to effective social betterment through public
programs lie not in the realm of policy theory, and if there is a historical
record of readiness of political authorities to innovate, then the nexus
of concern lies squarely within the field of political scientists' traditional
intellectual responsibility.

The causes of difficulties span substantive areas. They lie within the
implementation process, as it flows across policy areas and areas of
substantive concern.

Earlier it was noted, however, that of the three broad sectors of the
policy systems paradigm (output, implementation, impact), strategies
of research are the least developed in the implementation sector. That
is a bit discouraging. One cannot set out simply to assemble public
records and punch data that will be easily applied to test hypotheses of
known vitality (as it is argued here can be done to reasonably good
effect with regard to output research). If massive resources were indeed
available for high-powered implementation research, it is not at all clear
that the present state of the art would lead to such resources being
effectively used.

Rather, the highest research priority at present is to engage in careful,
guided induction. Sabatier and Mazmanian, for example, have provided
a checklist of implementation conditions that are prima facie attractive
and not wholly deterministic. Once a set of instances of successful policy

implementation is identified, the immediate task seems to be to isolate those attributes of service delivery which distinguish the successful cases from the blind alleys. This is in large part a task of literature collection and review, coupled with intensive, loosely structured conversations with participating administrators, followed by sensible coding of implementation attributes, many of which will fall within the available conceptual guidelines and some of which, no doubt, will be novel or situationally unique to national experience (Hofferbert and Ergüder, 1982).

One of the most obvious and theoretically critical questions is how far the Turkish analogy will stretch to other LDCs. Although the Ottoman Empire's experience was peculiar, it seems that the premature bureaucratization and the phenomenon of interbureaucratic competition is common in LDCs. It is probable also that the distinction between control and service will aid comprehension of these commonalities. And, finally, the chances are good that the application of the policy systems paradigm, in form if not in detail, will prove valuable in pursuit of such inquiry.

The burgeoning literature on the roots and routes of the welfare state has, to date, been consciously limited in its theoretical and empirical elaboration to the Western industrial democracies. It has, furthermore, been oriented principally to explanation and only loosely and subtly to intervention. We have here argued that these limitations are not entirely necessary. The paradigm of policy analysis seems exportable. From the standpoint of social utility, however, there is an apparent need to shift emphasis from causes of policy variance, on one hand, and consequences, on the other, to a more central emphasis on the intervening implementation process.

5

What Social Scientists Do Not Know about Public Policies in Poor Countries

This chapter argues that there are no universally, cross-nationally applicable prescriptions for modes of policy analysis. Rather, analytical tactics should be adapted to the policy priorities that exist in particular settings. There are patterns to such priorities, apparently as a function of level of development. Available policy analytic tools could be better fitted and adjusted to those priorities, especially to basic needs policies, the thrust of much development effort in recent years.

Much that is written about the condition of poor people in poor countries appears to be little more than a chronicle of tragic fate. To the extent that there is a clear effort at honest scientific explanation, the sorting out of causal linkages, there is little effort to array alternative causes according to their relative susceptibility to deliberate, goal-oriented change.

Scholars who should know better indiscriminately mix fate and geography, history and culture, human frailty and venality with domestic policies and external relations, all variously blamed for the misery of the Third World's poor. The misfortunes of being born in a particular locale and of having inherited a particular history or set of cultural traits and values are, to be sure, important contextual influences and constraints on the options for alleviating human misery. But neither fate nor geography, history nor culture, human frailty nor the world capitalist system are politically equivalent to specific policy options in their susceptibility to purposeful change.

We can build better policy research and thus provide better guidance for effective intervention on matters involving the poorest people of the poorest countries. We must begin by judging the quality of diagnoses according to criteria of scientific excellence rather than by the apparent promise of immediate impact. That is, we may have to judge the fruits of social inquiry about poor people in poor countries by the quality of questions rather than by the quality of answers. This is a morally uneasy stance.

Many items in the literature about the Third World often assert that there is growth without development. (See the excellent collection of essays in Seligson, 1984, for varying views of this assertion.) The claim is based on observations of extreme poverty persisting and income disparities often widening in countries that have nevertheless experienced rapid increases in GNP and other indicators of growth. For those who expected to see aggregate growth as the key to general betterment, this must be at least a disappointment. For many, it is a moral outrage (Goulet, 1977; Frank, 1978; Gran, 1983; Hope, 1984). If, however, the assertion is to be translated into questions for inquiry—Has there been growth without development? How much? Where? Why?—then a variety of derivative scientific tasks emerge:

- We must define the key concepts (growth and development) in empirical terms and then seek data for their measurement.
- We must catalog (and enumerate) the incidence of growth without development, development without growth, and growth with development. (A superficial examination of available data strongly suggests that such variance exists.)
- We must array alternative explanations of such variance in a manner that provides a credible test and accommodates plausible rival hypotheses.
- As policy analysts, we must ask specifically what share of the variance in that which is morally repugnant is caused by differences in public policies over which identifiable actors have some reasonable control.

A common assertion is that successful project implementation requires community participation in planning, implementation, and evaluation. Among social scientists concerned with effective intervention at the local level in the Third World, this statement is a near article of faith. I find it credible on its face and supported by substantial case material (e.g., Gran, 1983). Yet the frequency and vigor of its assertion are hardly matched by the persuasiveness of the evidence. At a minimum, such investigation should include the following questions:

- What are the various forms of participation—by whom, at which stage of project development and implementation, and in what tasks?
- Does the necessity and form of participation differ from one project to another? (For example, is participation as essential for a road project as for a community sanitation project?)
- How is "successful implementation" to be gauged? At what level of aggregation should it be measured? Over what time frame?
- What barriers, structural and cultural, must be overcome to maximize participation (e.g., sex roles, caste differences, local traditional authority structures) and at what cost?
- Are there saturation levels, for example in multiproject integrated development schemes, beyond which the pool of participants is exhausted?
- How much salutary participation can be achieved via the instruments available to policy makers?

By stating these questions, I am not by any means suggesting that the family of inquiry they represent is not well populated. The bibliographies of major aid agencies (UNDP, FAO, World Bank, AID, UNICEF, and others) stand as stark evidence to the contrary. Likewise, academic social scientists have entered the fray with vigor. (See, e.g., Frank, 1978; Murdock, 1980; Gran, 1983; Hope, 1984; Weede, 1985, for a diverse set of explorations well supported by extensive bibliography. See especially the bibliographic notes in Gran, 1983.)

Peculiarly sparsely represented among those applying the tools of empirical research to the plight of the world's poorest, however, are those political scientists who have in recent years adopted and adapted the craft of policy analysis. In the hope that this state of affairs will not be long-lived, I propose in this chapter to present a preliminary diagnosis and prescription for some general priorities in the application of policy analysis by social scientists (in general) and political scientists (in particular) to policy efforts in poor countries.

Global prescriptions are likely to be of limited value. Rather, my main argument is that *effective strategies for policy analysis must be attuned to the priorities of policies as they exist* in the countries in question. Different mixes of policies require different mixes of analytical tactics. A useful array of those tactics should rest on an examination of the mix of policies pursued in different contexts. In the next few pages, therefore, I will first explore the variations in policy priorities as they exist in countries at different economic levels and as they have changed over time. This will be followed by a taxonomy of policy analytic approaches fitted to those differences in policy priorities.

Policy Priorities and Economic Levels

Drawing on World Bank data, Figure 5.1 shows the percentage of central government spending devoted to five categories of policy activity, for two time points (1972 and 1986), arrayed by level of gross domestic product. The pairs of bars are for 1972 and 1986. A careful examination of the figure will reveal the general pattern of difference in priorities for countries at four levels of GNP per capita: The lower-income economies ($270 GNP per capita, 1986), the lower middle-income economies ($750 GNP per capita, 1986), the upper middle-income economies ($1,890 GNP per capita, 1986), and the industrial market economies ($12,960 GNP per capita, 1986). Excluded from the analysis are two other categories listed in the World Bank tables, the high-income oil exporters, because of their atypicality, and the East European nonmarket economies, because of lack of reported data.

The higher the GNP the lower the percentage of central government funds spent on general government (and "other," an unfortunate aspect of the World Bank classification scheme). The share for general government and other spending is highest for the poorest countries and drops steadily through the richest. This pattern probably reflects several simultaneous processes. One is likely economy of scale that can be attained beyond the bureaucratic infrastructure essential for the range of basic government functions. It may also index the proclivity of less developed countries toward bureaucratic bloat, with the public service acting as a source of patronage and a substitute for other forms of human services.

Unless there were a general negative secular trend in the overall size of government, which is clearly not the case, the economy-of-scale argument for differences in general government costs would predict a temporal decline in that percentage. Such, however, is clearly not the case for 1972 to 1986. That period, unlike the previous fifteen years, was characterized by widespread economic constraint, including two

Figure 5.1 Spending Priorities of Central Governments as a Function of Level of GNP:1972 & 1986

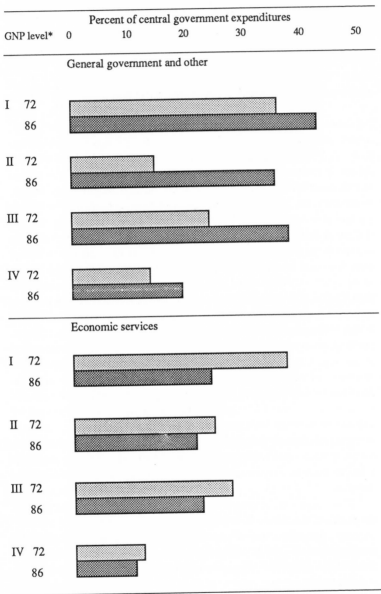

(Continued ...)

(Figure 5.1 - Continued)

Percent of central government expenditures

(Continued. . .)

(Figure 5.1 - Continued)

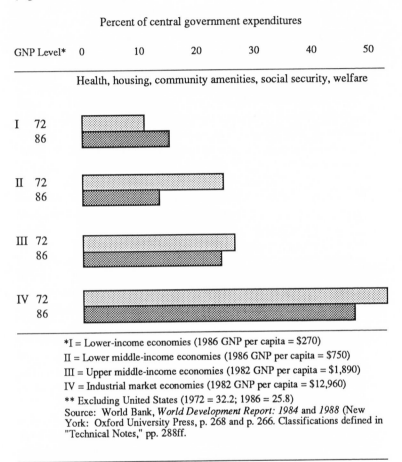

Percent of central government expenditures

| GNP Level* | 0 | 10 | 20 | 30 | 40 | 50 |

Health, housing, community amenities, social security, welfare

I   72
    86

II 72
    86

III 72
    86

IV 72
    86

*I = Lower-income economies (1986 GNP per capita = $270)
II = Lower middle-income economies (1986 GNP per capita = $750)
III = Upper middle-income economies (1982 GNP per capita = $1,890)
IV = Industrial market economies (1982 GNP per capita = $12,960)
** Excluding United States (1972 = 32.2; 1986 = 25.8)
Source: World Bank, *World Development Report: 1984* and *1988* (New York: Oxford University Press, p. 268 and p. 266. Classifications defined in "Technical Notes," pp. 288ff.

worldwide recessions, an oil price shock, and extraordinary inflation. Of all five policy areas, the general government category, at all levels of GNP, includes the highest people/things ratio. That is, a larger fraction of the funds goes for salaries and wages, as contrasted to buildings, equipment, and the like. Personnel costs are the least elastic component of national budgets. On the basis of this reasoning, one would predict that accelerated economic growth, as occurred widely in the late 1980s, would lead to reduced priority for general government. Eventually, in other words, the longitudinal and cross-sectional patterns should converge.

Infrastructural investments, under "economic services," occupy highest priority (after general government) among all but the richest countries. Right behind general government (and "other," unfortunately) are economic services. This is, perhaps, the least descriptive title in the figure. It includes "fuel and energy, agriculture, industry, transportation and communication and other economic affairs and services" (World Bank, 1988, 299). It is in this set that one finds investment in infrastructure and other functions directed principally at aggregate national growth. Such services occupy early priority, and they stay central until a very high income level is reached, with the only sizable decline occurring between levels III and IV.

Economies of scale are very much in evidence in economic services. Roads, bridges, power systems, and irrigation projects all are relatively durable, with much lower operation-capital ratios than other areas of policy. This is confirmed by both the cross-sectional and temporal data. Priority for economic services among the richest countries is less than half what it is for the others. And the pattern holds within income categories over time, with the percentage lower in 1986 than in 1972 for all four groups of countries.

Defense is the highest priority among lower middle-income countries, occupying lowest priority among the very poorest and the very richest. National defense is hardly a luxury, but it is beyond the effective reach of the very poorest countries. Yet military investments are made as quickly as the means become available, as seen in the dramatic increase in defense's share in 1986 compared to 1972 in the very poorest set of countries. The priority for defense, however, tops out at a relatively low level of GNP. Beyond a per capita GNP level of about $1,500, defense, relative to other policies, declines in priority. The pattern is consistent for the 1972 to 1986 period also, with the poorest countries increasing their defense priority while all others either held steady or declined.

Education gains the highest priority in the lower middle-income countries but declines steadily as GNP increases beyond that level. Education and defense, though not the absolute first priority, as indexed by spending shares, have very similar cross-level profiles. The level II countries (lower middle-income) show the highest priority for defense and education, but both decline at higher levels of GNP. I strongly suspect that each must be viewed from the standpoint of nation building: defense for protection and order; education for national socialization and human factor development. (Note that I have excluded the United States from the defense shares calculation because it peculiarly distorts the pattern among the other level IV countries, as reported in the note to Figure 5.1.)

Education priority, as a function of central governments, has a pattern similar to that of defense, except that the 1972 to 1986 period saw a reduction in the education share. There are several factors hidden behind this pattern. First, unlike defense, there is a substantial amount of subnational (provincial and local) spending on education, and this decentralization tends to rise with GNP. Poor countries have a tendency to centralize policy responsibility and especially a policy that is so central to the nation-building enterprise as education.

To the tendency of richer countries to decentralize finance for education must also be added two demographic processes at work in Figure 5.1, both cross-sectionally and longitudinally. First, birth rates are such that development has been accompanied by a reduction in the proportion of school-age children in the population. Second, there is a natural upper limit to the percentage of the population which are potential students. As a country approaches 100 percent of the age cohort enrolled, the marginal advantage of education over other policies declines. This process holds both cross-sectionally and longitudinally.

The share of expenditures for health and human services rises monotonically and dramatically up the economic development scale. Health and human services do not come up against such a natural ceiling as education, although there is evidence (not visible in Figure 5.1) of a general topping out in the 1980s among the richest countries. Human services grow steadily and nearly monotonically as one moves up the economic development scale. Seen the other way, human services receive the lowest share of the budgets in the poorest countries, increasing steadily through the richest. This is, perhaps, the prime target of critics of the priorities of poor countries and the emphasis of policy makers in the Third World on the trickle-down theory of development. More will be said about this feature of the data when I discuss basic needs policies a bit later.

Human services costs are apparently rather elastic. The monotonic rise in the priority for human services with GNP nearly matches the decline in priority for general government. Likewise, however, the apparent inelasticity of personnel costs in the latter, which yielded increased shares from 1972 to 1986, is matched by general declines in shares for human services over the same period. Although there is no mathematical lid (beyond 100 percent of budget) on the size of the human services clientele, unlike the case with education, the former policies are sufficiently elastic to be vulnerable during rocky economic times.

If we accept these figures as a reasonable reflection of the priorities of countries at varying levels of affluence, it follows that the policy analytic tools needed most among the poorest are those pertaining to government management, the technical evaluation of economic services, some attention to evaluation of education, and maybe, down the road a way, analyses of health and social services. (I beg the reader's indulgence if I put aside the question of defense policy analysis. That is a field unto itself and one in which I claim no expertise whatsoever. I did, however, think it worthy of note where defense stands vis-à-vis other policy priorities at varying levels of GNP.)

A Taxonomy of Policy Analytic Tools

My fundamental assertion is that an assessment of the broad national needs for policy analysis should be matched, again broadly, to the policy patterns and priorities of the country, setting aside for the moment any moral or ideological critique of those priorities themselves. As I have shown above, that patterning is, in large part, a function of the stage or level of economic development of the country. Many critiques of evaluation research, though perhaps generally accurate, fail adequately to tune criticisms to the fit of analytical techniques to policy substance (e.g., Garn's critique of cost-benefit analysis, 1983). To aid in this matching process, I offer a very preliminary taxonomy of analytic tools (with no effort at mutual exclusivity) for three of the major areas of policy activity depicted in Figure 5.1. Table 5.1 presents a first tentative effort in that direction.

Table 5.1 attempts to convey several messages at once. First, it suggests a classification of policy types or emphases which tap important variations across countries, even countries at comparable levels of economic development, but especially those at different levels. Each of these three policy areas is suggested to be directed toward different dominant standards or goals. The three "E's" of policy analysis, efficiency, effectiveness, and equity, are differentially relevant across the three sets of policies. Economic services are mainly to be judged by the return on investment, that is, efficiency (World Bank, 1988, pp. 41–78). Economic growth, though tricky, is more readily measurable than the multiple objectives of an education system.

Education policy certainly contains elements subject to clear efficiency assessment (e.g., cost of alternative design and materials for school buildings, alternative student transportation systems) but is less amenable than are highway policies to assessment in terms of quantifiable consequences. Efficiency is often traded for effectiveness in education. Beyond a very primitive level of basic mass education, cost is less central to assessment than gross effectiveness, however measured. Criteria for trade-offs between effectiveness and equity in education are more contestable. The relative emphasis on effectiveness versus intergroup or interclass equity of public education is very much in the forefront of disputation in most developed economies, suggesting that the effectiveness-equity criterion remains unsettled. In some contexts, demonstrated effectiveness of public education policy may be both necessary and sufficient as testimony of success, largely regardless of either efficiency or equity, at least within very wide ranges.

Effectiveness without equity considerations will hardly ever suffice as a standard of assessment for health and welfare policies, which are principally aimed at a central criterion of equity. Again, as with education, equity considerations do not displace concern for efficiency or effectiveness, but rather are added to those standards. The distinction can be appreciated, however, if one thinks of assessing government versus market provision of certain services. Least amenable to such contrasts are welfare programs. The presence of public health and social insurance schemes in this set, however, precludes ruling out such comparisons, thus broadening the span of alternatives against which the effectiveness and efficiency of health and welfare programs may be gauged. It is the equity consideration, however, which locks such functions, once assumed by government, into the public sector. The second set of entries in Table 5.1 concerns the goal clarity and singularity of

Table 5.1 Taxonomy of Policy Analytic Tools

	Economic services	Education	Health and welfare
Dominant standard ⟶	Efficiency	Effectiveness / equity	Equity / effectiveness
Goal clarity and singularity ⟶	High	Low	Medium

Policy Analysis Phase	Policy Analytic Tools		
Ex ante : Planning aids	Benefit/cost; simulation and forecasting; econometric modeling; linear programming	Cost/ effectiveness; needs assessment surveys; comparative analysis— program design	Cost/ effectiveness; needs assessment surveys; econometric modeling; comparative analysis— program design
Formative/ process analysis— performance assessment	Financial auditing; program review; "field reports"; PERT/CPM	Financial auditing; implementation assessment; utilization review; (case analyses)	Financial auditing; implementation assessment; utilization review; (case analyses)
Ex post/product— evaluation	Benefit/cost; economic impact review; aggregate "productivity"	Clientele surveys; aggregate comparisons of client benefit	Clientele surveys; aggregate comparisons of benefit and "productivity"

policies in each of the three sets. No policy has a single objective. And certainly none can be reasonably assessed without attention to indirect, perhaps unintended, effects. But the goals of investments in highways or hydroelectric dams are considerably more straightforward and focused than are the goals of a university system or a mental health program. In this instance, I posit that health and welfare goals occupy a middle position in terms of clarity and singularity between economic services and education.

The third and last dimension which I attempt to capture in Table 5.1 is the form and timing of policy analysis, with notes on the relevant tools at different phases of the analytical process. I divide the policy analytic foci into three more or less familiar phases: the ex ante, or prepolicy phase, seeking to aid prediction of effects and payoffs; the formative, or in the terms of Chapter 1, process analysis, which essentially addresses the attainment of certain planned steps in the implementation process; and the ex post, or, again in the terms of Chapter 1, product analyses, which attempt to assess the consequences (direct and indirect, intended and unintended) of policies and programs on social targets following implementation.

Along with other writers, I readily recognize that these are not entirely discrete spheres of analytical activity. Midstream evaluations, perhaps based on ex post tactics, may be used for projective decision making, in an ex ante fashion. Formative and ex post (sometimes called summative) evaluations may be conducted simultaneously for continuing programs. And so forth. The distinctions, however, are real, both in their differentiation of the questions that are asked and of the analytic tools employed.

I shall not engage in an item-by-item explication or defense of the particular tools suggested as fitting each policy at each phase of analysis. The list is meant to be suggestive. The essential point is that different arrays of analytical tools are appropriate for different policies at each phase of the process. And if less developed countries have peculiar policy mixes, they also need peculiar mixes of analytical tools.

One key area of recent policy development in LDCs, however, is very poorly accommodated by the typology. This is the category most commonly called basic needs policy.

As a particular focus for policy development, basic needs took on a special identity in the 1970s. The content and target of basic needs policies have resulted in their frequently being the focus of externally provided aid. Projects are also designed specifically not to be terribly costly in monetary terms. Therefore, a relative pursuit of basic needs policies is not adequately reflected in comparative spending patterns such as those summarized in Figure 5.1.

Policy Analytic Implications of the Basic Needs Strategy

My purpose in this section is to present neither a thorough bibliographic review nor a careful exposition of the history of the basic needs strategy (BNS). But my conception of the problem will be best appreciated if it is at least put in a bit of historical perspective.

The major thrust of development theory (mostly as written by Western observers or Western-trained citizens of LDCs) from the end of World War II until well into the 1960s was focused on the dynamics of aggregate national income growth, often indexed by GNP per capita or change in GNP over some specifiable period of time. Pejoratively identified as trickle-down theory, the policy focus was on infrastructure development (dams, bridges, irrigation projects, roads, factories—economic services in Figure 5.1), on the expectation that benefits would flow throughout the population in LDCs. W. W. Rostow is closely identified with the income growth policy position, but his is only one of the most widely cited treatments (1961). The income orientation took on more real form in the design of aid programs, the patterns of domestic budgeting in LDCs, and the form of development planning.

Concern existed all along about the assumption of trickle-down. Early anxieties about social equity were partially allayed by the work of Simon Kuznets, who posited the now well-known inverted "U" theory of income distribution, whereby early capital investment and infrastructure development would yield initial concentration at the top, from which redistribution would flow at a not-too-distant future date (1953). Figure 5.1 offers some support, but basic needs advocates challenge the acceptability of the implicit time frame.

For many observers, this strategy, however solid its empirical base, is distasteful (as contrasted to factually in error). Somehow lining the purses of traditional elites, with a goodly share spilling over into the profit columns of foreign (i.e., Western) corporations, all in the name of doing good for the poor of the world, was hard to accept. Improved data and research on income distribution also produced some empirical findings (albeit scattered), which failed to support fully the expectations of income growth policy, even when modified by the inverted U hypothesis. Patterns observed longitudinally in particular countries did not regularly bear out the predictions initially formulated on the basis of cross-sectional analysis (e.g., Goulet, 1977; Adelman and Morris, 1984). Cases such as the "Brazilian Miracle" came to be cited regularly to show that growth does not ensure reduced inequality of income (Evans, 1979).

By the early 1970s, the sometimes shrill accusations of persons readily identifiable as radicals came to occupy a respectable place on the policy discussion agendas of established organizations such as the Organization for Economic Cooperation and Development (OECD), World Bank, and AID. In particular, concern about the measurement of income distribution, as it affected the bottom rung of the ladder, and the fit of growth strategies to it drew increasing official attention.

The basic needs strategy moves beyond primary concern with either aggregate growth or income shares, however affected or measured, and focuses particularly on the absolute conditions of life of the poorest people in the poorer countries. If one were to graph the postwar intellectual and policy planning history, it would be something like Figure 5.2.

Figure 5.2   Priorities in Development Policy Planning: 1945–1985

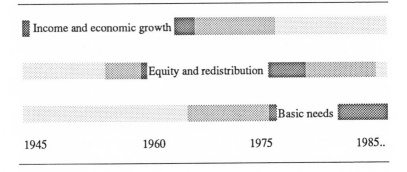

Since the 1975 amendments to the U.S. Foreign Assistance Act, which specified a shifting of focus more in the BNS direction, there has been a significant acceleration of interest by policy makers and scholars in the plight of the poorest of the poor (McGreevey, 1981, pp. 1–3).

What are basic needs? Paul Streeten, one of the principal spokesmen for a BNS, outlines it, rhetorically, as follows:

> The objective of the basic needs approach to development is to provide opportunities for the full physical, mental, and social development of the individual. This approach focuses on mobilizing *particular* resources for *particular* groups, identified as deficient in these resources, and concentrates on the nature of what is provided rather than on income. It is, therefore, a more positive and concrete concept than the double negatives like "eliminating poverty" or "reducing unemployment." It does not replace the more aggregate and abstract concepts which remain essential to measurement and analysis; it gives them content. (Streeten, 1979, p. 136)

In the content of the BNS literature, one finds a range of differentiation between normative and empirical concerns. Streeten, in particular, takes a hard-nosed approach to the specific shortcomings of the income orientation of earlier approaches to development, citing testable (and frequently tested) factors that interrupt the flow of the trickle downward (the most dramatic of which are the Swiss bank accounts of corrupt indigenous leaders). Basically, however, it rests on the inapplicability of the Marshall Plan theory to LDCs.

The Marshall Plan was significant in restoring preexisting physical facilities and market networks of Europe. It provided workplaces and tools for existing human capital. That human capital, along with the managerial and work practices that go with it, is virtually absent from many LDCs. And infrastructure has had to be built, not rebuilt.

Although sharing many of the moral priorities of most critics of the common patterns of income distribution in LDCs (and elsewhere as well), the advocates of a BNS focus on *absolute* conditions of privation at the bottom of the LDC totem pole. That Brazil's poorest had a smaller share of GNP after the "miracle" than before is less important for the BNS advocate than that many of Brazil's poorest experienced a substantial improvement in absolute income, health, literacy, and so on over the same period. That India's income redistribution favored the poor during the 1960s is less important to the BNS advocate than that India's poorest, along with most other Indians, may have been poorer in 1970 than in 1962.

A result of the overaggregated research orientation has been a lack of awareness of the marginal value of improvement in life conditions for poor people. One of the most popular indexes of income distribution, whose flaws are noted but which is used and abused widely nonetheless, is the Gini coefficient. It is one of the clubs with which many a development strategy has been bludgeoned. The construction of Gini, however, is such that unit differences in income are treated as identical up and down the scale. The result is that no weight is given to the diminishing marginal utility of income up the scale or, what is much more important, the vastly greater marginal utility of units of improvement in life conditions (including monetary income) near the bottom.

Where a summer hailstorm can mean starvation next winter—where life hangs in the balance of normal variance in natural phenomena—a gain that moves one from a life-threatened condition to a condition of minimum security is a tremendous marginal gain, however small the absolute value. Put, perhaps misleadingly, in monetary terms, to move from an annual equivalent of $200 income to $400 is far more than a doubling. It may be life-saving (see Scott, 1977). The basic needs strategy seeks to accommodate such differentials without losing sight of the equity considerations embodied in income distribution.

Some concern is clearly retained in BNS not only for income distribution but also for aggregate growth, in clear recognition that an equal piece of a big pie is bigger than an equal piece of a small pie. National autonomy, in terms of minimization of dependence, is also implicit in this basket of concerns. Although aid policies figure prominently in the BNS literature (see Streeten, 1979, p. 144), the aim is to avoid turning LDCs into permanent charity cases.

Not wholly worked out, however, is the theory of trickle-up, or what might be called the theory of capillary action, that is, the extent to which meeting basic needs of the poorest will redound to general economic growth and increasingly less difficult redistribution. The need for further conceptual development, data acquisition, and research in this domain is clearly recognized by the most rigorous writers in the field. Also recognized but hardly worked out is the question of the proper institutional setting for alleviation of basic needs. Streeten comments:

> For operational purposes, we must distinguish between three different aspects of the basic needs approach—supply, demand, and institutions. There must be adequate production or imports of the goods and services in question; there must be adequate purchasing power by the poor to buy them; and the organizational arrangements must facilitate access and delivery. The institutional framework has tended to be ignored in many conventional approaches [read "income-oriented"] to poverty elimination. In the basic needs approach, however, it is of crucial importance. Three types of institutions are important; basic needs are met by the market, by public services and transfers, and in households. . . .
>
> One reason why the basic needs approach is necessary to supplement the previous development emphasis on minimum incomes and poverty lines is that the income approach has tended to neglect the household and the public sector, which in turn has led to the neglect of basic needs where these sectors figure prominently. (Streeten, Foreword, in Leipziger, 1981, p.xii)

This would seem to be a call for the tools of political science (à la policy analysis, both process and impact) and anthropology in relatively greater doses than economics, at least at the margins of research. Exploration of data problems (see McGreevey, 1981) and conceptual difficulties (discussed below) reinforce this inference.

As in any field of research, there are in the BNS normative problems, theoretical problems, measurement problems, and data problems. I shall discuss these successively.

NORMATIVE PROBLEMS IN A BASIC NEEDS STRATEGY

How morally tolerable is (any?) apparent affluence in the face of visible human deprivation of basic biological (and psychological?) needs: food, clothing, dwelling space, health care, literacy?

There is an inability in the field to deal effectively with trade-offs of values possibly resulting from some perception of special rewards for special performance in the political economy (e.g., creativity, personal orderliness, efficiency, desire for opportunity, potential for mobility, hard work). How much protection should be given to those who do not try (or who have given up)? At the expense of those who have tried hard, often against awesome odds? How much difference in life conditions is too much, even if "earned" by some members of the community?

What weights attach to particular trade-offs? How much weight goes to building a road into a remote area so that health care can be more effectively delivered (e.g., refrigerated vaccines)? The road also aids the market and the potential distancing between formerly poor persons. The vaccines could be delivered to the most vulnerable by helicopter immediately, perhaps at lower unit cost if the cost of the road is amortized into the marginal cost of vaccinations. Such a line of reasoning does not lead to easy answers. But it is important to look toward the set of questions.

THEORETICAL PROBLEMS WITH A BASIC NEEDS STRATEGY

There is a lack of agreed conceptualization of second- and nth-order impacts (positive or negative) of varying degrees of maldistribution. Further, there is lack of differentiation between different forms of maldistribution, many of which may be trade-offs for one another, such as interclass (or interethnic) inequality, interregional (e.g., urban versus rural) inequality, intrafamily or household inequality (parents versus children), intergender inequality, and intersectoral (primary, secondary, tertiary; public versus private sector) inequality.

There is a good deal of awareness in the literature of the need for trade-offs and that they must be accommodated in any supermodel of a basic needs strategy. A commonly cited case is the deprivation of infants dependent on breastfeeding when opportunities for remunerative employment for women rise. Such opportunities increase women's economic significance, raise family gross income, expand psychological horizons for women, create new chances for exploitation, and destabilize families, in addition to removing the milk supply.

There is unclear specification of cultural and socioeconomic contextual factors such as caste or clan that ameliorate or exacerbate inequality. There is frequent citation of literacy policy, human resources policy, nutrition policy, housing policy, but rarely any specification that could facilitate measurement or operationalization, even if the data existed.

MEASUREMENT PROBLEMS IN BASIC NEEDS STRATEGY

To some extent, the BNS reduces the magnitude of the analytical problem relative to the frequency with which people talk past each other about what is development. When applied to the relevant subpopulation, the Physical Quality of Life Index (PQLI, a composite index of infant mortality, life expectancy, and literacy), for example, is easier to conceive, compute, and communicate than the array of more aggregate-oriented terms and measures (factor cost, production function, and the like) (Morris, 1979). Always implicit and often explicit, however, in the BNS literature is a concern for psychological and social aspects (correlates? causes? effects?) of minimal well-being.

Important but dreadfully unclear are what attitudinal and social network measures should be employed. There is little confrontation (in the economic literature, at least) of trade-offs between communal or familial coherence and self-perceived individual choice or freedom, for example. The concepts are recognized and listed but not accommodated systematically. Any analyst who fails to note such trade-offs thereby guarantees his or her later ability to claim that a particular policy or program failed. The summary literature is rife with such cheap shots (e.g., Todaro, 1981).

The dependent variables of an economic growth model of development, the conditions by which relative success or failure are to be measured, include changes in GNP per capita, the ratio of manufacturing to agricultural employment, level of factor capacities, import-export ratios, debt, and terms of trade. The independent variables are wide-ranging but normally include net national investment (foreign and domestic), technical education capacity and production, infrastructural capacity (transport, communications), and related matters.

An income distribution or social equity model focuses on income shares, Gini coefficients, and patterns of consumption (luxury versus subsistence commodities) as dependent variables. Change in GNP per capita, penetration of multinational corporations, concentration of trade, and other indicators of dependency are the independent variables.

Research in both the economic growth and the social equity modes relies primarily on nation-level aggregate data for testing of key hypotheses. Models in both realms tend to be heavily weighted toward economic indicators. Minimal attention is directed toward systematic testing of the impact on policy accomplishment of variance in political processes or modes of service delivery.

A basic needs strategy sets as the dependent variable a range of indicators of quality of physical and social life at the bottom of the socioeconomic ladder. Housing conditions, literacy, infant and child mortality, health status, and dietary intake all index degree of attainment of basic physical needs. Likewise, leisure time, self-perception, sense of independence, perceived freedom, and relations among neighbors suggest the range of factors that reflect (if not identify) basic social and psychological needs.

Although research approaches are still evolving, the most promising independent variables that are subject to purposeful change are likely to be priorities across alternative projects, level of investment in projects, modes and levels of community mobilization and participation, and variations in methods of service delivery. This list, of course, does not address those community and individual conditions which must be held constant if policy and project impacts are to be measured effectively.

DATA PROBLEMS

The data needs for testing hypotheses derived form the linkages between the independent and dependent variables of a BNS model are dramatically different from those employed in either of the two previous models. A test of central propositions of BNS cannot rest on nation-level aggregate data. Ideally it requires village- and household-level data. With the exception of some cost-accounting information, such data are virtually never gathered and maintained on a routine basis.

Many experts are skeptical of the cost-effectiveness of survey data among the poorest populations in poor countries. Sites are inaccessible. Residents are suspicious of or subservient to outsiders. Essential base material (such as a population enumeration for statistically reliable sampling) are unavailable. Facilities for proper analysis (coding staff, computing equipment) are distant or absent (Moris, 1981). I am unconvinced by this skepticism. For certain projects, I cannot conceive of any better way to gauge impact than to ask the people who are supposed to benefit from the projects. Rather than an insurmountable barrier, I see an opportunity and challenge for the design of appropriate research technology that may require reassessment of customary criteria of data purity in the interest of greater net knowledge (see, e.g., M. Hofferbert, 1985).

A generation of statistical talent and effort has gone into the improvement and standardization of aggregate socioeconomic data, collected directly for administrative records and inferred from reasonably well-tested models. The shift to BNS rolls back the clock on the relative adequacy of data. A first-rate treatment of conceptual problems and the specifics of data inadequacy (and citations of some of the best that there are) is McGreevey and his contributors (1981).

The data problems, however, are not unrelated to key conceptual and theoretical difficulties. For example, we can consider the dramatic difference resulting from measuring personal income in terms of exchange rates versus international prices. By the former (1970) Kenya = $144 per capita; India = $98 per capita. By the latter, Kenya = $275; India = $342.

Vital statistics are reliable inversely to the poverty of a country. The poorer the country (or the more poor people in a country), the less likely the poor are, proportionately, to be enumerated. Yet the logic of BNS is to address their particular problems.

As a consequence of data deficiencies, we are unable to assess accurately the form and magnitude of basic needs requisites, test the differential effectiveness of specific programs and projects designed to implement a basic needs strategy of development, or decide between alternative administrative or procedural tactics at the local level (see R. Hofferbert, 1985).

Until there are concrete administrative purposes for basic needs data (such as the purposes specified in the 1975 U.S. AID legislation; McGreevey, 1981, pp. 2–3) they will be collected ad hoc. The most widely advocated ad hoc method is the household survey. (For example, compare victimization surveys with the Uniform Crime Reports in the United States.)

Collection and refinement of statistics follow the policy agenda. The requisite statistics for BNG, especially household surveys, are presumed by some to be too costly. Resources expended for their collection are assumed to compete with other worthy tasks. Data will be gathered when there is a perceivable administrative or political need. Already the attention being given to BNS is stimulating a reassessment and reform of time-series data collection, at least in some countries (see bibliography in McGreevey, 1981).

Conclusion: Analytical Tools for Basic Needs Policies

Several observers have already noted the need for a novel conceptualization of evaluation and analysis of basic needs policies and projects, proposing variations on locally based, participative research (see, especially, Gran, 1983; M. Hofferbert, 1985; R. Hofferbert, 1985; see also Blaikie et al., 1981; Alberti, 1981). In Table 5.2, I suggest some analytical tools for basic needs projects, following the categories presented in Table 5.1.

In adjusting analytic tools to specific policies, I am trying to avoid such overgeneralization as Guy Gran's condemnation of cost-benefit studies. Cost-benefit analysis need not be and has not consistently been an instrument of oppression or exploitation. It may, however, fit economic services far better than education, social services, or basic needs.

Although I challenge some of the global assaults on any particular tools of analysis, I do accept the challenge of scholars such as Gran, who advocate a fundamental change in the manner in which some policy analysis should be done in specific places and substantive domains. Particularly, I have elsewhere offered a critique of existing policy analytic practices. I offer a revised (revisionist?) approach to evaluation of basic needs projects (R. Hofferbert, 1985). I suggest that there is a role for the barefoot evaluator. Local people can be trained in the essentials of effective data collection and reporting for process and product evaluation. Examples exist that can be exploited and upon which informed improvements can be made (see M. Hofferbert, 1985).

The World Bank is the major sponsor of some of the most significant research on service delivery mechanisms in the Third World. And yet, even within the corpus of admirable evaluation research executed by the bank, one finds rarely, if ever, a systematic inquiry into the specific consequences for the quality of poor peoples' lives of variance in service

Table 5.2   Analytic Tools for Basic Needs Policy

Dominant standard ——————➤	Efficiency / effectiveness / equity
Goal clarity and singularity ——————————➤	Low

Policy Analysis Phase	Policy Analytic Tools

Ex ante—
  planning aids
	Needs assessment;
	feasibility studies;
	participatory planning;
	comparative program
	  design

Formative/process analysis—
  performance assessment
	Community surveys;
	field reports;
	PERT/CPM;
	implementation
	  assessments;
	utilization review;
	financial auditing

Ex post/product—
  evaluation
	Household surveys;
	cross-community
	  control group
	  comparisons;
	utilization review;
	time-series
	  follow-up

delivery procedures and mechanisms. That is, the literature is dominated by case studies, with very little attention to or even seeming awareness of the need for comparative analysis of implementation procedures and practices (see, for example, Weiss and Jequier, 1984; Paul, 1982).

The role of the academic policy analyst in such policy areas as basic needs projects at the village level is to design novel, appropriate research technology, fitted to the people and projects involved. We may also engage in training of field personnel and local participants in the evaluation process. But we must abandon the model of the large-scale, externally imposed and funded, one-shot ex post product evaluation if we expect our talents to serve the needs of emerging priorities among the poorest people in the poor countries of the world.

6

Bottom-Up Development Research, Illustrated by the Case of Domestic Water Systems in Nepal

Where's the variance? I've worked intensively on four water systems over three years. Recently, I've inspected another twenty or so to assess maintenance problems and needs. Of systems constructed under the same overseer, half will be working and half will be broken.

Nothing changed in Kathmandu is going to change that. It's the wrong place to look. You've got to look where the variation is, and that's most at the village level.

The next question, of course, is, Can you change anything there? Maybe reforms in Kathmandu are all you can do. Maybe the variation at the village level is all cultural.

I spent my first three months in Umagau doing *nothing* on the water system. Not a stone was moved until an experienced overseer arrived. He got diggers by lying to the people, told them they would be paid. They started digging and eventually finished a rather poor, ten-kilometer system. Didn't seem to mind the lie much.

Those first three months, I learned Nepali, built an outhouse, and basically felt like a fool.

That was a Chetri caste village—pretty high.

Two years later, I went to Toli, a Magar village. They are still Hindus, but lower caste and Tibeto-Burmese-speaking ethnic group. The morning of my second day there, sixteen porters took off (on a three-day walk) to Surkhet to get supplies; another dozen volunteers started digging.

Is it culture, or did I do something different?

—Mark Hofferbert

As noted in the previous chapter, the central normative and empirical tendencies of development theory and research have shifted and evolved over the years since World War II. Presumably, a major purpose of

109

development research, and especially that by political scientists, is to anticipate, prescribe, and evaluate the relative effectiveness of alternative public policy thrusts for the development process. Most research, prescription, and disputation by social scientists (especially political scientists, sociologists, and economists) has focused on fairly global or highly aggregated concerns. Both theory and measurement strategies comport with that macro level of analysis.

Since the early 1970s, however, a major strategy designed into multinational and bilateral assistance policy, as well as the more or less autonomous policy activity of particular poor countries, has been consciously aimed at micro impact. This is particularly true of the basic needs strategy.

As noted in Chapter 5, BNS does not deny the legitimacy of concern for aggregate national economic growth, distribution, or dependency. But it emphasizes policies that address down-to-earth living conditions of the poorest people in poor countries. Of top priority is getting enough for people to eat and drink and providing basic sanitation and housing.

The BNS also faces such ancillary concerns as appropriate technology for subsistence agriculture, irrigation, low-level crop innovations, and reforestation. The priority of basic needs has long defined the central focus of UNICEF. It has risen on the agenda of other specialized multinational agencies. As discussed in Chapter 5, U.S. aid has been mandated since the mid-1970s to address basic needs in program design. The World Bank has taken the lead, both in strategy and policy tactics, in setting basic needs strategies.

The discourse of many academic development theorists, however, has persisted mainly at a macro level. It requires no denial of the relevance of debate over macro processes (e.g., world systems analysis, dependency theory) to call for an effort by policy analysts in the relevant social science disciplines to include the processes and consequences of the basic needs strategy on their agenda of inquiry.

This chapter adds further volume to the call for such a revision of the agenda. It does so in an unorthodox way. Rather than the customary tools of empirical social inquiry, it offers a combination of travelogue, autobiography, and ethnographic research (to give a fancy name to a report on a visit to some very poor people in a very poor place).

In 1981, our son Mark Hofferbert joined the American Peace Corps, taking up duties, after three months' training, overseeing construction of domestic water systems in the middle hills of Nepal. In 1983, my wife, Rose, and I spent a few weeks with Mark on his job sites in some relatively remote villages in the Dailekh district. It was a rare opportunity, in the company of a person experienced in the culture and language, to go places, meet people, and see things that normally are hard to include in the experience of a political scientist. Anthropologists do that sort of thing routinely, but they ask a different set of questions than does a political scientist.

It would be presumptuous of me to believe that academic colleagues really want to read about my trip to Nepal, or to learn what a fine kid I have, or even to learn how tough my wife and I are in facing uncommon levels of inconvenience and discomfort. I approached the visit, however, with a systematic objective. I wanted to get initial guidance on answering two questions: (1) Does anything work in the effort to improve the lot of some of the poorest people in the world? (2) What information would a policy analyst need to help get answers to the first question?

The balance of this chapter relates a series of vignettes, selected from notes based on our experience in Nepal, which illustrate the circumstances attendant to implementation of basic needs policies, in this case, principally the construction of domestic water systems.

I have no idea how typical this case is. Since it was not my first trip to a poorer country, however, I did see some similarities to other places. And I know that projects of the scale of those in which my son was engaged are being pursued in hundreds if not thousands of sites around the world at any given time. The political science literature in general and the policy analytic subcomponent of it in particular seem singularly unaware of that activity. That unawareness is reflected in the level of analysis and the priorities of questions being asked by persons concerned with development.

To clarify some of the references in the narrative vignettes, I will describe the place where all this took place.

The observations made here are based on a visit of a few weeks during May and June 1983 in and around the districts of Surkhet and Dailekh, in the area called the Middle West of Nepal, roughly one-third of the way across the country from the western border and about one-third of the way north from the southern border with India. The nearest place likely to be accurately represented on a map is Nepalgang, the border town to the south. The terrain is very rugged, being almost entirely mountains (hills in the vernacular of people who can look north on a clear day to the Himalayas), with valleys a few hundred feet above sea level, rising to heights of four to eight thousand feet.

Surkhet is a town of about two thousand with some electricity and a small rice mill. There is a grass landing strip served irregularly every few days by a Royal Nepali Airline Twin Otter. "Jeepable" roads are open about eight months a year to Nepalgang and (since early 1984) to Kathmandu, the latter being about fourteen hours by truck under ideal (nonmonsoon) conditions.

Surkhet is a rather primitive place, but it serves as an administrative headquarters for various development projects. From Surkhet foot trails lead out to the villages in the hills. A very old, traditional trail from India to the Tibetan border passes through Surkhet. We spent several days on that trail. Surkhet has a British Save-the-Children clinic, a United Missions leper colony, and assorted public offices and supply depots.

Aid volunteers from various countries (especially the United Kingdom, United States, and Netherlands) congregate in the town between extended on-site jobs in the remote villages. We spent a few days there on either end of a trek to some of the sites where our son worked.

The first site we visited, a two-day hard walk into the hills from Surkhet, was a tiny village called Khadkabada, where Mark was supervising construction of a domestic water system. From there, we hiked a few days further into the hills to another district capital, Dailekh. Dailekh, being in the mountains and inaccessible except by animal, foot, or helicopter, is much more primitive than Surkhet. It has no electricity, a very unreliable water supply system, frequent food shortages, and other privations. Both Surkhet and Dailekh sometimes appear on maps available in the West, although only their approximate location is indicated. Khadkabada is not on any map.

Aside from walking, there was not much to do with my time, so I kept fairly extensive notes. I discussed my notes with Mark and other volunteers on the rare occasions when we met any others in the hills or, more frequently, in Surkhet.

In most of this chapter, I use very little specialized social science terminology. I respect our jargon for its ability to shorten what would otherwise take a lot of everyday words. What I want to convey here, however, is adequately and clearly conveyed by common English. I respect our abstractions, and I respect our desire to neutralize the passion of our inquiry. But I find everyday language more useful for discussing daily human concerns, especially moral concerns. I have tried very hard to be objective in my reporting, yet I have made absolutely no attempt to disguise my moral preferences or values. The topic is ill-suited to such a divorce, in any event.

I am calling for a policy analytic focus on basic needs strategies as at least an adjunct to our current scholarly foci. To convey what such a policy analytic focus would involve, it is necessary, in a few cases (e.g., my discussion of water system construction) to go into detail. I hope the reader will appreciate my motives.

Water System Construction: An Example of Appropriate Technology

APPROPRIATE TECHNOLOGY

Today, among persons interested in improving the life of the little folks in less developed countries, we hear a good deal about appropriate technology, which is another term for simple improvements. The philosophy gets a little romanticized sometimes, as in Ernst Schumacher's *Small Is Beautiful* (1973) or the nostalgic rhetoric of the Greens in West Germany, when they relax. The appropriate technology I have seen is not necessarily beautiful. It may be nothing more than a minimal compromise with necessity.

Those who pursue the design of appropriate technology try to maximize two objectives. First, they try to design tools and methods that use locally available material, or at least to avoid depending on material that has to be bought and transported from other places. This is a matter of both money and community independence. There is unquestionably a philosophy of seeking to maximize community independence. But it does not require a weepy commitment to the wee folks and their lovely culture to see a reason for it. Most really poor places are also, for one reason or another (usually geography), hard to get to. So if you want to improve water resources, irrigation, tillage, health practices, construction methods, or any other targets of appropriate technology, you had better not create dependence on material that has to be bought and hauled in. If you are in a place where bamboo grows wild, consider using it for pipes rather than carrying in PVC. If there is nothing locally to serve as a pipe (and people excrete in all available open waterways), you need to import something that reaches a reasonable balance between cost and durability.

It is not necessary to buy the romance to see the argument for cost-effectiveness in stressing community independence. If developing improved techniques for meeting basic needs also keeps poor folks out of the clutches of the multinational corporations and home-grown capitalist demons, that's a bonus.

There is another objective of appropriate technology that requires a little more taking on faith than the idea of community independence. This is the goal of adapting innovations maximally to existing practices. It rests on an assumption that *some* long-standing practices that look stupid may be pursued for subtle but sound reasons. Primitive tillage, for example, preserves the crumb structure of the soil, which is vital if the available rainfall is to be retained. One does not have to accept the functionalist arguments of anthropologists lock, stock, and barrel to see something to this line of reasoning. It is a variation on the adage "If it works, don't fix it."

Most of the world's poorest folks live off the land. They are nomads or subsistence farmers. The latter grow or make virtually everything they have. They grow their grain and save it somewhere to eat while the next crop is growing. If they are lucky, they keep some domestic animals that can be dispatched every now and then for meat.

An amazingly small number of poor peasants in the Third World have deep freezers. Not very many of them even have a stock of Mason jars. Storage of both grains and meat is a problem. Vegetables, if they are used to eating them, are not so bad, if there is water available. Most of the world's poorest people live in warm or hot places, where vegetables can be grown much of the year if water is available.

Grain storage is a tragedy and illustrates the potential of appropriate technology. Current estimates are that 25 percent of India and Nepal's grain rots or is eaten by rats. Some tribes' dietary rules are such that they can eat the rats so it's not a total loss. (I haven't seen comparative studies of the return in basic nutrients of eating the grain versus eating the rats that eat the grain versus eating some other critter that eats the grain and/or the rats such as a rat-hunting pig.) Some United Nations people have designed a grain bin that is virtually rat-proof. Instead of storing the grain in a covered bin with no floor, it is stored in a bin constructed on posts, with a floor, and inverted tin funnellike things around each of the posts. The tin funnels are made of used cans, a readily available commodity. The rats won't climb the posts over the funnels. It is pretty neat but not widely used.

Another example is the "smokeless chullo." Most Nepalese keep their mud ovens (chullos) going all day long. The oven is inside the house or at best inside a three-walled room. There is no chimney. The incidence of respiratory maladies among the Nepalese is awful. Researchers have developed a smokeless chullo, using the ideas behind airtight stoves in the West, coupled with a cheap chimney (though still requiring metal or clay pipe). It requires no more technology, except for a few feet of stovepipe, than the current version. Not only will it eliminate most of the smoke in the house, but it will cut fuel consumption to 30 percent of its current level.

An island is emerging in the Bay of Bengal composed of Nepal's topsoil. In the early 1980s conservationists estimated that Nepal's trees would all be gone by the year 2000 at the rate of wood consumption and population growth in 1980. Cutting to one-third the amount of wood burned in the chullos would make a tremendous contribution to forestalling disaster.

The idea behind the improved grain storage or the smokeless chullo is to introduce practical devices that do not seriously challenge current practices. In any event, appropriate technology is technology that does not require excessive or undue changes in current practices. It recognizes that the peasant may be smarter than he can verbalize. Of course, addressing maximum improvement for minimum change also recognizes that the peasant is often stubborn. Peasants are stubborn for good reason.

Peasants cannot afford to take risks. At least in the places we visited in Nepal, they were living at the very brink of survival, on both sides of that brink. A hailstorm (during the period when the grain pollen is loose), half an inch less rain, a sick bull (needed for plowing), or any of a host of other misfortunes could mean a dead baby next season. These people have virtually no cash. They have no reserves except family. But in isolated villages, there is no cumulation of surplus at all, by anyone. There is no "ever normal granary" or "friendly society" that can absorb shocks.

How can one expect such people to be risk takers? How can one expect them to accept the arguments of some gringo or college boy who tells them that putting in carrots and sacrificing some of the rice space will be better for them when no one in the village has ever before grown carrots? Or how does one convince them to plant a new strain of rice that may, under ideal conditions, increase yield but does not taste right to them?

If one takes into account that village lore often contains stories of some enterprising person who did accept advice to change, only to be left holding the bag by an inept government agency or to be victimized by unforeseen variables, one begins to see good reason for reluctance to change.

This is not to say that these peasants are stupid or that they cannot learn. Every development worker who has spent time in the field can tell stories about dramatic changes in behavior, especially when appropriate technology was well fitted to the local situation. Small investments in hygiene education seem to bear large returns.

When surveys are taken, however rudimentary the methods used, it turns out that the peasants of the hills of Nepal put water systems among their top priorities. It is not clear to me that this ranking is based on a realization of the benefits of sanitation as much as on an expectation of reduced work load. The women, in particular, seem to be fans and supporters of the people who are building water systems. After all, it is the women who must carry the water. It is not uncommon for women to spend hours daily carrying water in jugs on their heads or backs.

CONSTRUCTION METHODS

There is plenty of water in Nepal. It is not there all the time, but a lot flows through and falls on this little country. The Himalayas are not a true divide, in the sense that water west of the Rockies flows to the Pacific and water east of them flows to the Atlantic. There are several massive gorges through the Himalayas that bring water down from the Tibetan plateau. In annual rainfall, the high Himalayas are quite arid. But rainfall in the middle hills is ample. When the north-south rivers are added, there is a goodly flow through the country.

Unfortunately, both the Himalayas and the middle hills are rocky, making drilling for groundwater impractical. In the Terai, along the Indian border, there is a substantial supply of groundwater, and most water development projects there rely on dug or drilled wells.

In the hills, however, the most practical method is a gravity-feed pipe system. Since the entire countryside is steeply eroded mountains, nearly all of the hill dwellers are within one or another form of watershed. A source of flowing water can usually be found near the top of any given ridge.

The initial task for those building gravity-feed water systems, therefore, is to identify a source that is clean (free of animal or human pollution at or above the spot), ample in volume for the villagers below, and not currently claimed by someone immediately below it for either household or irrigation purposes.

To find pollution-free sources it frequently is necessary to go to high places some distance from the villages. The volume of flow must be adequate for the population. Since land tenure rights are rather crude here, the question of claims on flowing water is often dependent on delicate negotiations, in which Mark was often involved.

At this stage I am skipping over all the steps of planning, administrative, and community policy and politics involved. The point here is principally the technology. But none of it works unless the social aspects are carefully husbanded.

At a suitable source, a stone and concrete collection tank will be constructed. Water will flow into the tank from the source. The tank has a concrete lid on it, which is locked. It also has a set of valves on the outside, in another concrete box, which is locked. The method of construction is simple but sturdy. The locks are to prevent tampering by people who would want to draw off the water for their own use, thus interrupting the flow to the villagers below.

Much of the technology is aimed at preventing tampering or damage by people and animals. The assumption is not that the people are malicious but that they do not have a sufficiently developed sense of mechanics to understand the consequences of cutting a pipe with an ax to provide a little water hole for the buffalo or bulls.

Cement must be carried in. To bring cement to Khadkabada, it was necessary for a porter to make a three-day round-trip, carrying a fifty-kilogram sack of concrete (the porter probably weighs around fifty kilograms himself). For that he gets about three dollars worth of rupees. If the project calls for a hundred bags of cement, there will be a lot of three-day trips and a lot of money in the community.

The porters are recruited from the village that will receive the water. They get paid upon return to the project site with the materials picked up in Surkhet. Of course, they have to eat along the way, which may require a little money. Mark would, on rare occasions, advance the men ten rupees (seventy cents) for the three-day trip, but he quickly discovered that the word spread and then everyone wanted an advance and began to bargain over how much. If word got back to his superiors, Mark would be in trouble for mishandling the funds.

We frequently saw mule trains on the trail, although they were obviously very long-distance caravans. They are also expensive since they must carry some of their own feed because of the minimal amount of forage along the trail.

At the time we were in Khadkabada, Mark was hopeful of completing the system before the monsoons. His bottleneck was portering up the cement. I asked him why he didn't use a mule train. He explained that the cement comes in fifty-kilogram bags. A man can carry fifty kilograms. A mule can carry seventy-five kilograms. The cost per kilogram is the same. But to use mules would require that the bags be split and put into two smaller bags (to come up to seventy-five kilograms and the mule loaded evenly on each side). And there were no extra bags. So they had to use men instead of mules. Also, of course, using men provided employment for the villages, an added benefit of man over beast.

Sand is carried from the nearest river valley, also by paid porters. In this case, however, the porterage may be done by local women as well as men. In the case of the Khadkabada project, sand could be acquired by a one-day round-trip walk.

Gravel is made on-site, for which some compensation is paid. This is usually women's work. They simply break large stones into small ones. Again, though technically simple, it is a lot of very hard work to get enough for a twenty-cubic-meter reservoir tank.

From the source tank, a large (approximately two-inch) galvanized pipe emerges and enters a one-meter-deep ditch. From there, the water flows downhill through approximately two-inch black plastic pipe. The black plastic pipe has also been portered in on somebody's back. It comes in very clumsy reels about four and a half feet in diameter, weighing about thirty-five kilograms.

The ideal drop rate is about 2.5 percent. The average source, in Mark's experience, has been located about six to eight kilometers from the main population concentration. This means digging a meter-deep ditch for about four to six miles, around the rim of a valley.

Mark uses an altimeter to measure drop. Every sixty meters of drop, it is necessary to install a break-pressure tank. This is another concrete box (about a cubic yard), which has a toilet-tank-like float valve in it, which allows water to come back to atmospheric pressure without overflowing. The plastic pipe can take only about sixty meters of drop, or "head," worth of pressure.

The method of assembling plastic pipe is interesting and illustrates the appropriate technology approach. In the United States, PVC pipe is connected by means of a double female union, held together by a special cement. One cannot rely on a continuing supply of connections or cement in the certain event of needing to repair a plastic pipe in the Nepalese village. An alternative technique is literally to weld the pipes end to end without any fittings. This requires a bit of practice and skill, but not too much. Three related tools are needed: an iron griddle that looks like a skillet without sides, a teflon sleeve that fits over the griddle, and a special chalk that melts at a particular temperature.

To join the ends of the pipe, the griddle is heated in an open fire, to the point that the special chalk will melt when touched to the griddle. Then the teflon sleeve is slipped over the griddle to keep the plastic from sticking. One person holds both ends of the plastic. The griddle with its teflon mitten is inserted between the ends, which are pressed against the griddle. As soon as the plastic flows, the griddle, with the teflon sleeve over it, is pulled out and the now-molten ends of plastic are pressed together. After fifteen or twenty seconds of pressure one has a permanent union, as strong as or stronger than the original pipe. It requires no expensive, hard-to-get glue and no fancy fittings. The only expendable item is the special chalk, and an experienced technician can estimate the temperature of his griddle without the chalk.

A site needs to be selected above the village for a reservoir tank.

When we were in Khadkabada, the initial digging for a twenty-cubic-meter tank (the biggest Mark had built) had been completed. Actual construction was to begin when the cement arrived.

The technique for constructing the walls and top of the reservoir tanks is called ferro-cement construction. It is the same basic technology used in the West to build concrete boats. It is also a nice example of appropriate technology. Apparently the basic method for applying it to village water reservoir tanks was developed in Indonesia.

The goal is to get a strong tank, requiring minimal maintenance, that can be built in a simple manner with cheap materials. That means avoiding heavy forms and expensive reinforcing material. The process begins with digging and smoothing a form out of the ground for the base of the reservoir. It is critical that large stones and irregularities be removed. Wire mesh and reinforcing rods are laid out, and concrete is poured over them to form the bottom and base for the sides of the reservoir. (The same technique used for the floor of the reservoirs is used to make slabs for outhouse floors so any experience gained in one setting can be drawn upon for the other, another reason for using local employees, if not actual volunteers.)

Once the poured concrete reservoir floor has set, side construction begins with installation of a wooden brace, not unlike a ferris wheel on its side. A series of arms come from a central hub. These hold vertical boards in place. Around these vertical boards (eight in a typical system), one wraps coils of black plastic pipe to produce a stacked coil of black plastic pipe, held in place from the center by the ferris-wheel-like device. The plastic pipe is part of the form. It will later be removed and used for branch lines throughout the community.

Around the coiled plastic pipe is wrapped light mesh wire (chicken wire) onto which a fairly rich mortar mixture is troweled. At specified intervals, vertical reinforcing rods are mortared into the structure, which is plastered up to an inch or so thick. Not too much is required but a good deal of care and supervision, lest weak spots be left in the walls of the reservoir.

This material constitutes the outer shell of the reservoir. After it has set well, the inner form (the ferris wheel device) is removed, as is the coil of plastic pipe, leaving a one-inch outer shell. The same process of plastering is repeated on the inside, yielding a two-to-three-inch-thick reinforced wall.

Construction of the lid is almost as simple and equally effective. The Indonesian-designed wooden spiderlike form allows for a coil of plastic pipe over the top, aided by reinforcing metal, plastered over outside and then inside, after removal of the pipe. A significant hole is left in the top of the lid. A large lockable trap door is installed in the lid because it is necessary for someone to be able to get inside periodically to clean the reservoir.

Mark says that everything has to be locked to avoid vandalism, but he is quick to note that the interpretation of vandalism is broad. He thinks he has detected a positive correlation between the education level of the village and the incidence of tampering with the water system equipment. The brighter they are, the more curiosity they have about such things. So they break it open to see how it works.

At the time the floor is constructed, a set of pipes and valves is installed. Required is an intake pipe, a clean-out pipe and plug, an overflow pipe, and an outlet pipe. All of these have appropriate valves. Heavy galvanized iron pipe is used. Valves are concentrated in a single lockable box outside the reservoir. When installing the pipes in the concrete floor, one must be careful that the pipes are strongly anchored so they will not crack the reservoir and all of the zinc galvanizing has been removed at the point where a pipe passes through the concrete, or the concrete will not adhere, leaving a leaking spot.

The key to successful installation is that all of the fittings be lined up in such a manner that they can be assembled in the valve box without cross-threading and consequent leaks.

Downhill out from the reservoir tank, branch lines (about one inch in diameter) are installed in ditches and extended to various sites around the community. UNICEF and His Majesty's Government policy guidelines call for the first tapstand to be at the school. Much negotiation goes on to determine where the rest of the tapstands will go.

A tapstand is a vertical pipe, often embedded in a stone or concrete base, with a valve on it. It is important that tapstands be located on a slope to allow drainage away from the tapstand. Commonly, drainage is channeled away a few dozen yards, at which point a simple earthen dike is built in a semicircle to create a watering pond of the overflow. If the slope is sufficient and the pond far enough away, animal wastes and water-borne insects will be kept away from the tapstand.

These are the basics of construction. Obviously, there are many little tricks in making sure the system is both efficient and durable. How to accommodate best to a particular terrain and how to select the best reservoir site are determined from experience. Mark indicates that he was not very proud of his first system but is confident of the quality of later ones. Part of that confidence comes from experience with the people, part from experience of a technical nature.

The principal role of the Peace Corps volunteer is to ensure proper mechanical installation, manage and dispense funds, order supplies, and, most important, harangue the diggers to get the ditch deep enough. The major challenge of these systems is not getting them into the ground but keeping them functioning. The soil is loose and rocky in this region. It is difficult to dig, but the soil is easily eroded or knocked away. So especially at places where there is likely to be erosion or animal traffic, it is vital to get the pipe deep in the ground. Frost is not a worry in most places but damage by people or animals is. Rarely is it possible to convince community volunteers to dig a whole meter deep.

Once, while we were in Khadkabada, we came upon a newly installed branch line that was already exposed at the edge of a deeply rutted trail. The first time a water buffalo walked by, he would kick and break the line, which was nowhere more than about six inches deep. At that point, Rose and I got an insight into Mark's mode of interaction with folks in the community.

He admonished a man nearby, who had apparently been responsible for the insufficient digging. In strong terms, Mark indicated how inadequate the installation was. He threatened not to allow the water to be turned on unless the ditch was deepened. At this stage, several women, including the poor peasant's wife, came on the scene. They promptly joined Mark in haranguing the victim. Shahiji, the technician working with Mark, joined in, but as the nice guy. It was a variation on the nice cop–tough cop routine, with Mark making the threats and Shahiji indicating that it would be in the best interest of the peasant to comply. Mark illustrated his point by grabbing the plastic pipe and pulling it out of the ground for several feet, then walking away visibly disgusted. Three hours later, when we passed by on our return walk, the peasant had completed relaying a good percentage of the pipe, under the critical and watchful eye of several women.

Why the tough stance? Would not a more gentle approach have worked? Mark says not. For his first year, he tried cajolery. It simply did not work. Apparently, if you are to be accepted as an outside expert, you have to carry yourself with authority. I was somewhat embarrassed by the scene. We always brought the boys up to be especially courteous and inconspicuous in foreign countries. And here was our kid playing the Ugly American. But it was hard to judge unless one can assess the results over a long period, which Mark has apparently done.

A bit of commentary on the division of administrative and fiscal responsibility is in order here. Materials—pipe, fittings, cement, tools —are purchased by UNICEF. Mark was recruited and paid by the Peace Corps but reported to the Ministry of Panchayat and Local Development (MPLD). The UNICEF field engineer, however, apparently had de facto supervisory authority over Mark, as did the district development officer and field engineers of the ministry. With funds provided by the government through the ministry, Mark was responsible for hiring, supervising, and paying all employees on the project, principally masons and porters. In theory, all digging was done by local unpaid volunteers. Overall, it is a managerial mess, but, as is not uncommon, it is to be expected because of the shared responsibility of participating entities.

The major long-run bottleneck is availability of community volunteers to dig the ditches. Villages apply, through the *panchayat* system, for a water system. At that time, an overseer (who may be a foreign volunteer or a Nepalese engineer) conducts a feasibility study, estimating the likely source, length, and other characteristics of a system, were one to be installed. (During the two Peace Corps terms he served in Nepal, Mark conducted several such studies.) Meetings are called of community members, at which time agreements to provide a certain amount of labor are signed (usually with a thumbprint from the stamp pad which Mark carried for that purpose).

Usually a couple of years or so pass after the feasibility study before anything further takes place. But once construction begins, the labor for digging determines the rate of progress.

Many UNICEF and MPLD personnel urge abandoning community participating and hiring paid diggers. Apparently projects have moved much faster when diggers were paid. Mark argues, however, that if they are not built by the people themselves the systems will not be maintained. This is an appealing argument until one confronts the delays involved in relying on volunteers. It's planting time; it's harvesting time; it's monsoon; it's always an inappropriate time for getting out in the broiling sun and digging a three-foot-deep ditch with an eighteen-inch hoe.

Here is another example in which a simple field study could test a very important hypothesis.

Respiratory Conditions

One of the most oppressive things about village Nepal is the constant hacking and spitting. Tuberculosis is rampant. Children are barefoot with their fingers always in their mouths. Especially in the morning, as the Nepalese wake up in the town or village, the air fills with a chorus of coughing, hacking, and spitting. Virtually everyone has lung congestion. If they laugh, their chests rattle like that of an old chain-smoker.

UNICEF is conducting a drive for the construction of smokeless chullos, clay cooking ovens with controlled draft and chimneys, which would also reduce destruction of trees and erosion since they burn 70 percent less wood than the chimneyless versions.

Some of the lung problems may be the result of communicable disease. But most of the coughing and congestion surely comes from the cooking smoke, in addition to the susceptibility it creates. Further, the only available wood is soft, green brush. Some people have their ovens on the porch, but most squat over them inside. They provide some heat in the worst of winter, though the temperature rarely drops much below freezing at night in this region. Not only are these inside ovens un-healthy, but they represent a very inefficient use of scare wood and the labor to collect it.

Locals argue that the smoke in the ceiling (under thatch, which is hardly that classy English reed stuff but simple wheat straw or grass that must be replaced every couple of years) creates a creosote that discourages termites and other bugs. I suppose the functionalists would love that.

Looking across the valley, one can spot the villages by the spindly trees. Lower limbs are broken off for wood and all but the topmost leaves stripped for fodder. Mark once described Nepali women as "a pile of leaves sprouting legs." It is quite a sight to see one of them climbing twenty to thirty feet up a tree trunk, swaying in the breeze, slashing off branches of leaves, which then are formed in an enormous bundle, twice the size of the woman, and carried off on the back from a strap across the forehead, the *namlo*.

Changing Styles of Local Leadership

In most villages (*panchayats*) the mayor (*pradhan panch*) is elected largely on the basis of being a good talker. This has been the traditional skill that seems to pay off. Volunteers, by and large, have a low opinion of these fellows. Their main objective seems to be to make sure that they get a water tap near their house.

In one of Mark's villages, the main work period on the water system coincided with local elections. One fellow, with no prior political involvement and not much of a talker, became active in the water project. He served on the water system committee and was elected *upa pradhan panch* (vice-mayor). Another man was elected *pradhan panch* (mayor) on the basis of his organizational and oral skills. He was able to motivate villagers to help throughout the construction of the system. Whenever Mark needed volunteer diggers, this man showed up, on time, with cousins, brothers, and neighbors.

Without the project, there would have been no occasion for these organizational talents to become manifest and visible. The net effect is to redefine the criteria for leadership. In the future, such criteria will be part of the political process in that village.

This illustrates a long-term sociopolitical side effect of cooperative development projects. The theory would be that such changes survive, redefine the criteria of political leadership, and, perhaps, have a multiplicative effect, showing up in other projects such as community health stations or reforestation.

Vasectomies and Related Snippets

Hikmet is a local health officer. It is a terrific job. He gets about 600NR (about $40) per month, mostly to pass out condoms and try to talk people out of reproducing. He has one wife and two children. He points out to other villagers that they had only two children (no deaths) and that they are clean because, with only two, his wife has time to keep them clean.

Mark notes that there is a limit to how much Hikmet can preach to his neighbors. Most of them are relatives. Can a fellow, anywhere, go up to his uncle and lecture him on his sex life? Yet when we met Hikmet, he told us of their most recent vasectomy camp. Apparently, the word is passed that a doctor will be at X place on Y date to give free vasectomies. (The doctor has to walk in, just like everyone else, although on rare occasions doctors are flown in by helicopter.) Often the doctor does not come on the assigned date, thus making many people walk (perhaps for days) for nothing. This uncertainty has created considerable skepticism and more than a little discouragement among health officers such as Hikmet. But this time, a couple of weeks ago, 110 men came on one weekend and got snipped. These folks can and do respond when given half a chance and a minimum of the right circumstances.

Migration

We frequently encountered whole families on the trail, always going in the direction of Surkhet. Mark indicated that they were migrating from the hills. Surkhet is a new regional capital, and apparently the word has spread that it is the promised land. It is a pretty paltry promise, if you ask me.

Not all the migration is permanent. Much of it is seasonal. Many people from Dailekh District also have land or homes in Surkhet. They travel between Dailekh and Surkhet according to the agricultural season and availability of labor. Some better-off families send one or two school-aged children to Surkhet for their education.

Surkhet valley, like the entire Terai over the ridge to the south, was malarial until recent years. Thus it was not inhabited except by a few risk takers or by those few people who were immune to malaria (apparently including the Tharus, a very interesting, reclusive, matriarchal tribe of the valley). Now that malaria is virtually gone and the more or less motorable road is in, it may become a bit of a center of opportunity.

An additional consideration, for those who tilt toward the cynical, is the question of how "they" managed to eradicate malaria. What has been the social and economic impact? How was the program administered? Financed? What was done for and to indigenous groups, however few they may have been (e.g., Tharus)? It would be a nice study of a program that worked.

Vaccinations versus Roads

With the push for basic needs by the World Bank and others, much of the debate in the development literature has been over the relative efficacy of building infrastructure, which is presumed to have economically multiplicative effects, versus services more immediately relevant to rudimentary well-being of the poorest people in the poorest countries. Big jobs such as dams and highways are seen as evidence of the (perhaps not disproven but certainly much maligned) trickle-down approach. That approach asserts that if you invest in big things, first it provides immediate employment, and second it provides economic growth. Even if there is some initial concentration of profit in a few hands (including, perhaps, foreign contractors paid with foreign aid), eventually the benefits will flow outward and downward.

Given the visible current misery of so many people in very poor countries, one can see how there would be aversion to infrastructural investment, especially if it seemed to benefit currently privileged groups (including multinational corporations) disproportionately. That aversion may well be based on no research or demonstrable long-term evidence disproving the efficacy of trickle-down but rather on a simple human desire to "put first things first." If people in those hills drink clean water, the incidence of the major child-killers should be reduced. Thus the thrust toward basic needs: water, housing, minimal health care, literacy. One need not be a raving hater of everything corporate to find that line of reasoning appealing.

Alas, the choices are not so clear-cut. As I often observed, Mark's effort to build safe drinking water systems was time and time again frustrated by the awful difficulties of getting the least bit of material transported in this pitiful place. The mountains simply refuse to lie down flat, regardless of the compassion of the person seeking to cross them.

The case of measles vaccine illustrates the dilemma. Measles is second only to diarrhea (a generalized term for a spectrum of gastrointestinal ailments, usually related to waterborne parasites, resulting in death most immediately from dehydration) as a child-killer out there. We know how to prevent measles: vaccination.

Poor places are usually poor in part because they are off the beaten track and hard to reach. I do not know the precise figure, but I would wager that 20 percent of the population of Nepal is more than a two-day walk from the nearest electricity. Consequently, they are more than a two-day walk from the nearest refrigerator. Measles vaccine must be refrigerated.

Vaccine can be delivered to the hills within a two-day walk of the nearest refrigerator by using an insulated cooler. But then either the people have to walk to the cooler at a specific time or let their children get measles. Even a primitive set of jeep trails would save most of those lives.

Current research (by large Western corporations) is aimed at designing better, lighter containers that will keep things cool longer and vaccine that will keep without refrigeration.

I find it interesting how many times, back home, when I mention the ease with which it would be possible to save the lives of many of the children who now die, otherwise humane folks will point to the perhaps far greater problem of overpopulation and, if there are no other listeners, ask if we really want to save all those kids. I must admit the legitimacy of this argument. Plagues and even wars are no longer doing the job they once did. My response is that birth rates go down with increases in infant and child survival plus literacy. I know I read that someplace. I surely hope that the research upon which those figures are based is better than most that is published on the Third World. Infanticide by inactivity is a damned repulsive policy.

In any event, is the question really vaccines versus roads? Is the trickle-down theory wrong? The more I see out there, the less interesting I find the usual dimensions of discourse on problems of poor countries. Which is more important, vitamins or protein? That is a ridiculous question.

I guess the most irritating aspect is the extent to which affluent academics and their allies (journalists and other analysts in and out of officialdom) have latched onto one or another "theory" of development as a way of catering to their ideological whims. After being in Nepal, I find those conversations not only dull but downright immoral. How dare these Mercedes Marxists exploit helpless people so they can make cute points among their fellow salon radicals!

I have no answers as to what constitutes the most effective set of priorities. I suspect that it varies a good deal depending on local conditions: geography, ethnic mix, place in the international cockfight, and so on. But I am confident that my awareness of the absence of easy answers is as well developed as anybody's.

Many development planning treatises assert that the first priority should be pure drinking water. At the time of our visit, Mark had given two years to building drinking water systems. When I asked him if he accepted the thesis that water ought to be first on the list of basic needs, he responded: "I don't know." That, for my money, was the most informed judgment I have heard yet about development priorities in the poorest places. One should not underestimate the experience and information that went into that "I don't know."

Vaccinations or roads? I don't know.

Conclusion?

As a treatise on the problems and prospects for bettering the lot of the poorer people in the world, if I have a main theme in this chapter it is that there are no conclusions and that one ought to distrust people who offer them. I suppose that is a conclusion of sorts. Maybe it deserves elaboration.

I said earlier in the chapter that the simple question I asked on the way to Nepal was, Does anything aimed at helping really poor people in really poor countries work? Judging from what I have seen in or read about Nepal, it's a hit-and-miss process. What fails once may succeed with another try. What succeeds once may be a dismal failure next time. But if you give up, you stop hitting as well as missing.

Statistics are nearly useless except for recent years, so it is hard to look at the figures and say for sure that anything is getting better. There does seem to be some progress on literacy, infant survival, and life expectancy, although Nepal is still far back in the pack. I distrust all figures on income distribution, partly because I can't imagine where the data would come from and partly because income is hard to gauge in a predominantly subsistence agricultural-barter economy.

If you asked me if there should be a Green Revolution in Nepal, with possible problems of dependency on imported fertilizer, possible tendencies toward concentration of landholdings, and other problems, I would have to answer honestly that I haven't the slightest idea (but not from having failed to think about it). I surely would have a hard time opposing *anything* that would increase net food or capital flow in the country, but I would also hate to see what little daily freedom their isolation and lifestyle affords to the folks in the Midwest eroded by economic regimentation. My opinion? I have no opinion.

Does anything work? Malaria is just about gone. WHO had a lot to do with that. So did His Majesty's Government. Roads are being built here and there. Some have been built by Nepalis alone; others have been built with aid and direction from India, Britain, China, the United States, or the Soviet Union. Here and there are hospitals, of sorts. Hikmet says that 110 men showed up at the vasectomy camp.

There are some numbers that show some improvement. It is reported that between 1965 and 1985 the percentage of primary school–aged females enrolled in school increased from 4 to 47. The United States did not do it so fast. Life expectancy may be pushing into the high forties. But the numbers are shaky. Even if they are true, how much is attributable to public efforts and how much to something else?

Would dismantling the world capitalist system improve the lot of the people of Khadkabada? Now? In twenty years? Ever?

Is there a battery of administrative reforms that would increase the impact of existing output and effort? Now? In a year? Ever?

Would a nearby road attract good teachers to Khadkabada? They could get to town on weekends. Would it attract young engineers so that some experience could build up in the area?

Would abolishing the monarchy, instituting competitive parties, and other reforms reduce the backbreaking, mind-numbing work load of the women of Khadkabada? Now? In twenty years? Ever?

Should the young men of the Middle Hills lay down their tools and take up guns? Would their sacrifice and that of those who get caught in the fray of a guerrilla war be recompensed? Does the record of guerrilla-aided national liberation movements provide sufficient evidence to warrant emulation? I have looked through some of the literature, and I cannot find an answer that meets even minimal standards of scientific credibility. Sure, there are stories about Cuba, good and bad.

There are anecdotes about Nicaragua. But the intellectual drudgery of coding and arranging data to serve genuine scientific curiosity rather than the predispositions of propagandists has not been devoted to the job.

Many books have been written about development administration, nearly all by people who spent most of their time in national ministries. After reading and teaching a bit of development policy, and after the trip to Nepal, I have gotten a little clearer not on what I *know,* but at least on what is reasonable strategy for *learning* something useful.

Clearly the knowledge needed is more social and political than technical. There is a job out there for political scientists and policy analysts. But they might get a good case of the green-apple two-step. (I lost twenty-five pounds in two weeks on the trail.)

If I had my way, I would let social scientists into the capital cities of poor countries only one day for each thirty they spend sleeping on the ground or floor in a village without running water, a road, or electricity. We need what I have come to call ''bottom-up policy research'' in poor countries. Somebody who can keep good notes needs to learn the right questions to ask and to ask them of the host of volunteer aid folks coming in from the field (that's how to spend the one day in the capital).

After we left in June 1983, Mark signed up for a second tour. For doing so, he got a month's home leave. In the course of his home leave, he was kind enough to be the featured guest at one of our brown-bag lunches at the SUNY-Bingamton Center for Social Analysis. A lot of graduate students and political science faculty came for a very informal discussion. Mark talked briefly about the technology and the administrative, financial, and social organization of water system construction in the Midwest of Nepal. Mostly, he took questions rather than delivering a full-blown lecture. Some of the questions were about personal existence, the Peace Corps, and such topics. Most, however, were pointed in the same direction as my policy reflections in this chapter. Priorities for project implementation was one significant theme.

One colleague asked him: ''Mark, if you were the absolute dictator of Nepal and had millions of dollars, what would you do?'' The immediate response was ''Build roads.''

At that, I was taken aback. It sounds like AID and the caricatures of Rostow put forth by all of Rostow's critics who have not read his work.

It sounds like trickle-down. You can't eat a road. Roads screw up the ecology. Roads make foreign contractors rich. Roads, by bringing in outside goods, information, and other things, are instruments of neo-colonialism. A year earlier, when asked about vaccines versus roads, Mark said he didn't know. Now, without a moment's hesitation, he says, "Roads!"

"Why?" my colleague asked, bemusedly thinking Mark had set himself up.

> Well, first, because that's what the folks out there say they want. Ask them, "What do you want most?" and they usually put roads near the top of the list.
>
> That's a good reason in itself. They're not stupid. They understand a bit about markets. I know a village that grows terrific tangerines but rather poor apples. There is another village a hard walk away that grows great apples. With a road, they could have a market.
>
> Now, I know that some of the money would go to truck drivers from India, but there would be a net gain for the farmers.
>
> Then there is the medical care and health services business. Right now, they are almost nonexistent. Roads would change all that. Education, for example, needs roads, not just for construction materials and supplies, but to attract decent teachers.
>
> Sure, they will disrupt the culture. But the culture is no longer eco-logically sustainable anyway. So the question is not change versus no change, but change that averts disaster.

To learn something that might help people making policy plans, I asked Mark where the points were for most useful social science focus. Mark replied:

> Where's the variance? I've worked intensively on four water systems over three years. Recently, I've inspected another twenty or so to assess maintenance problems and needs. Under the same overseer, half the systems will be working; half will be broken.
>
> Nothing changed in Kathmandu is going to change that. It's the wrong place to look. You've got to look where the variation is, and that's most at the village level.
>
> The next question, of course, is, Can you change anything there.
>
> Maybe reforms in Kathmandu are all you can do. Maybe the variation at the village level is all cultural.

I spent my first three months in Umagau doing *nothing* on the water system. Not a stone was moved until an experienced overseer arrived. He got diggers by lying to the people—told them they would be paid. They started digging and eventually finished a rather poor system. Didn't seem to mind the lie much.

Those first three months, I learned Nepali, built an outhouse and basically felt like a fool.

That was a Chetri caste village—pretty high. Later, I went to Toli, a Magar village. They are still Hindus, but lower caste and Tibeto-Burmese-speaking ethnic group. The morning of my second day there, sixteen porters took off for Surkhet to get supplies; another dozen volunteers started digging.

Is it culture, or did I do something different?

Another theme of the questions was the social impact of external interventions such as the installation of the water systems.

"What is the most likely impact of a water system in a village?" asked a colleague.

"Saving of time for the women, since they won't have to go so far for water."

"What will be the impact of more free time for the women?"

"I haven't any idea, and I doubt that anyone has studied it very systematically in Nepal," responded Mark.

"Wouldn't you want to claim that the health improvements would be the greatest benefit, given that so many diseases are waterborne?"

"I don't expect any noticeable health impact," Mark answered. "Most of the so-called waterborne diseases, particularly the parasites, actually are so omnipresent in the environment that our water systems won't make much difference. People shit all over the place. Then they walk through it, some time later when it is no longer physically visible. They pick their toes, handle food, and get sick. It's in the air, the bugs, everywhere."

My colleague persisted: "But surely you have some insight into the likely social change introduced by outside intervention. What *happens* when you finish a water system?"

Mark: "We usually cut a goat and get drunk."

PART III
The Disciplinary Mix

Among domains of social inquiry, policy analysis is a shining example of an interdisciplinary endeavor. Yet the call for cooperation among disciplines within the academy is more often an admonition than a celebration of achievement. That there are elements in the analysis of the causes and consequences of government policies and programs which use the talents of diverse disciplines is beyond question. The implicit sense of inferiority frequently encountered in the writings of political scientists engaged in that effort testifies to the need for guidance across fields of expertise. That economists, sociologists, and substantive experts (e.g., health, education, environmental, or agricultural policy) so commonly talk past each other should urge us toward a clearer specification of tactics for cooperation.

Chapter 7 attempts to enumerate some such tactics. I address the "loneliness of the long-distance policy analyst" by noting that it is not only across disciplines that mutual awareness of policy analytic tactics is lacking but within the work of leading political scientists themselves. Some attention is given to explaining the atomization of policy research, as well as to particular avenues of focus that might bring about a bit of salutary cohesion.

The theme of the division of labor is sharpened for political science in Chapter 8, which raises the possibility that policy analysis, as it has been practiced, may not be an appropriate major undertaking for political scientists, as students of political system performance. I suggest that the problem is one of choosing and identifying dependent variables. Political scientists are eminently qualified to examine factors that affect *politics,* as such, and particularly *democratic* politics. They may not be so good at assessing the impact of public policies on those elements of society commonly stated as policy goals. I expose myself as an unabashed, old-fashioned liberal, who takes a pretty unequivocal stand for the advancement (and even the export) of systems of popular control, call them "democracies," "polyarchies," "representative systems," or whatever. Prescribing for that advancement, on the basis of our very best, most rigorous modes of inquiry, is a moral objective I hold to be worthy of the efforts of my discipline. Far from abandoning policy analysis, however, I argue that it is a vital and as yet unexploited strategy for advancing understanding of how democracies are built and sustained.

7

On the Division of Labor in Policy Analysis, or, The Loneliness of the Long-Distance Policy Analyst

Policy analysis seeks to understand and explain the causes and consequences of what governments do to and for the people. As noted in Chapter 2, the strategies and tactics of policy analysis are ever more centrally featured in the curricula of academic programs in political science and public administration. Training persons to understand and explain the causes and consequences of government actions is an eminently interdisciplinary endeavor. The assertion of the interdisciplinary nature of the task, however, is more often symbolic than substantive. This chapter attempts to highlight the commonalities of concern across the disciplines and subfields engaged in policy analysis.

I suggest that there is a view of the task which makes clearer the content and implications of engagement in common tasks by members of the several policy analytic subfields and disciplines. The disciplines and subfields engaged in policy analysis are distinguishable more by their particular conception of independent variables than by methodological peculiarity. Each specialized focus tends to explain policy on the basis of historical, economic, social, and political characteristics which are central to the long-standing foci of that discipline. Rather than recognizing the need to exchange foci and to incorporate in systematic fashion the competing explanations offered by related disciplines, the practitioners of each tend to view that which is outside their particular explanatory priority list as residuals or simply error terms, thus saving a great deal of listening and reading time.

Maximization of understanding and minimization of intellectual parochialism in policy analysis can be advanced by a focus on the degree of controllability of factors influencing variations in the form and impact of public policies. A focus on controllability does not require a major overhaul in the work habits or methodology of anyone now engaged in policy analysis. Rather, it seeks a modest but very consequential adjustment in styles of discourse.

That adjustment is required, however, not only across disciplines as they are traditionally organized but also within the one with which I am principally concerned—political science—for intradisciplinary noncommunication is at least as severe as it is across disciplinary frontiers.

Intradisciplinary Noncommunication

In preparing these observations, I more or less arbitrarily pulled from my bookshelves seven volumes with the word *policy* in their titles. There was a bias because I was a visiting professor abroad at the time and had paid my own postage to ship the books. Therefore, I must have thought they were pretty good. All but one or two were written by people who call themselves political scientists. I was curious about the degree to which they cited one another. Table 7.1 lists the books and the results of my foray into bibliometrics. (Read across the rows to see who is cited by the authors listed in the left-hand column.) Authors get credit for citing *anything* by the other authors, not just the specific books listed. Thus, for example, that in his *Speaking Truth to Power*, Wildavsky does not index any of the other authors really is not fair of him since only two books on the list totally ignore him. What message does this table convey? First, it says that a lot of scholars with a lot of years in the business take no formal cognizance of one another's writings. Hofferbert might be forgiven for batting only five hundred since his is the oldest book on the list and he thus lacked the opportunity to cite several of the others. Mayntz and Scharpf might be similarly forgiven but more because they are across the sea than because they had no opportunity to cite the other works. Perhaps Stokey and Zeckhauser, the economists, can be forgiven because they are economists. But none of these excuses are convincing because nearly everyone on the list has a long history of publications in previous books and in numerous conspicuous professional journals. Thus there was ample opportunity for cross-citation.

Most of the authors cite themselves fairly often. Dye, Sharkansky,

Table 7.1 Who Cites Whom? *or* The Loneliness of the Long-Distance Policy Analyst

S&Z - Stokey and Zeckhauser: *Primer of Policy Analysis* (1978)
(Decision methods—economists)

AW - Wildavsky: *Speaking Truth to Power: The Art and Craft of Policy Analysis* (1979)
("State of the art" book—political scientist)

HHA - Heidenheimer, Heclo, and Adams: *Comparative Policy Analysis* (2nd ed., 1983)
(Cross-national comparisons by substantive areas—political scientists)

M&S - Mayntz and Scharpf: *Policy-Making in the German Federal Bureaucracy* (1975)
(Process analysis; one country—political scientist/ administrationists)

TD - Dye: *Understanding Public Policy* (5th ed., 1984)
(Text: Comparative analysis—political scientist)

IS - Sharkansky: *Public Administration: Policy-Making in Government Agencies* (4th ed., 1978)
(Text: Comparative analysis—political scientist)

RH - Hofferbert: *The Study of Public Policy* (1974)
(Text: Comparative analysis—political scientist)

Who   **Cities Whom?**

	S&Z	AW	HHA	M&S	TD	IS	RH	Score
S&Z →		N	N	N	N	N	N	0
AW →	N		N	N	N	N	N	0
HHA →	N	N		N	N	N	N	0
M&S →	N	Y	N		N	N	N	1
TD →	Y	Y	N	N		Y	Y	4
S →	N	Y	N	N	Y		Y	3
RH →	N	Y	N	N	Y	Y		3

and Hofferbert cite each other a good deal, but they also cite others in the set fairly often. The comparativists (Dye, Sharkansky, and Hofferbert) thus seem the most eclectic of the set, with each of them citing each other, plus something by Wildavsky, and Dye citing Stokey and Zeckhauser.

These observations are not meant as condemnation of particular practitioners of policy analysis but rather to show the atomization of the field.

Definitions and Alternative Approaches

Public administration and public policy training programs are being established and refurbished in many countries. The Dutch government, cooperatively with the European Community, established the European Institute for Public Administration in Maastricht. The Institute for Advanced Studies in Public Administration (Institut de hautes etudes en administration publique) in Lausanne, Switzerland, matriculated its first postgraduate students in 1982. The examples are not confined to the industrialized West, as seen in the efforts, for example, of Boğaziçi University in Istanbul or the University of Tel Aviv in Israel to launch comparable programs.

New institutions and established ones seeking to maintain currency invariably must face a fundamental challenge: what is the appropriate mix of multi-, intra-, inter-, and cross-disciplinary talents and what are the linkages between and across them that produce, first, a coherent and useful curriculum, and, second, a critical mass of talented scholars who will be likely to stimulate and fertilize one another's research endeavors?[1]

Put another way, is a particular institutional collection of scholars merely a fortuitous aggregation, at risk of becoming a cacophony? Or is it a cohesive unit, with the promise of being a symphony?

Professors usually assume, by way of self-protection, that there is an implicit coherence to their various pedagogical activities and that the brighter students will surely sense that coherence. Yet only rarely is the fundamental question of the division of labor addressed among representatives of the relevant disciplines. And as Table 7.1 suggests, communication problems are intra- as well as interdisciplinary.

POLICY DEFINED

There are many fancy definitions of *public policy*. One which is reasonably trouble-free, if semantically unsatisfying, I gave earlier: that which governments do to and for people.

POLICY ANALYSIS DEFINED

From that simple starting point, *public policy analysis* may be defined as the effort to understand the causes and consequences of variation in public policy.

Mention must be made of an old and often abused distinction between *basic* and *applied* policy analysis. It is not so important to refine the distinction as to indicate the linkages across the two aspects.

Basic policy analysis is concerned with seeking to maximize the variance that can be explained about the policy process (usually macro or comparative).

- Goal = Maximum generalizability
- Advantage = High chance of external validity
- Disadvantage = Low chance of internal validity

Applied policy analysis as concerned with (I have not come up with a short, crisp way to say this, but it is very important to the argument here) identification of malleable components of the policy system such that one can locate "leverage points" that, if changed, will have predictable consequences for the targets of policy (usually micro or case study).

- Goal = Maximum fit to specific conditions
- Advantage = High chance of internal validity
- Disadvantage = Low chance of external validity

There is no fundamental conflict or competition between basic and applied research. (And there is no necessary reason for a trade-off between internal and external validity; it just works out that way in practice.) I see no problem in the same person being engaged in both, perhaps simultaneously. There are, of course, practical differences between research stimulated by scientific curiosity and that stimulated by the terms of a contract or the needs of a client. (See Chapter 2 for some of the professional and career difficulties.)

A potentially very happy marriage, however, is possible, and it is important to articulate it in a discussion of the division of labor in policy analysis. The marriage of basic and applied research is consummated when policy systems models identify general constraints or resources while also specifying the most effective levers for particular circumstances.

One of the lessons of comparative policy analysis in its quantitative, aggregate incarnation is that it focuses attention on ranges of choice by explicitly identifying social, economic, and cultural limitations on the alternatives faced by policy makers. It highlights the conflict between determinism and the latitude for volition among policy makers.

How much of that which determines variations in policy (across time or across jurisdictions) is a result of immutable forces and how much of changeable elements of the process (Hofferbert, 1974, chap. 8)?

In his 1943 volume *The Hero in History,* the late Sidney Hook brings home clearly the message that public policy is both the deeds of leaders and the product of processes. The deeds may reflect a *Weltanschauung.* The product of processes may reflect a *Zeitgeist.*

An essential task of the policy analyst or adviser to the prince(ss) is to identify the opportunities for choice, either in the selection of deeds or in the design of processes, which tip the *Weltanschauung* and bend the *Zeitgeist* toward human betterment. In that task it is rare that the learning of the counselor will be superior to the wisdom of the prince(ss), even less so when the prince(ss) is in office because (s)he embodies that least "learned" wisdom, the wisdom of common people living day to day with the consequences of their own morality.

The analyst as counselor is akin to a pilot, taken onto a ship as it enters harbor, to aid in navigating a few shoals in a narrow strait. The pilot commands neither captain nor crew, but (s)he offers, nonetheless, guidance which is ignored only at grave collective peril.

And many academics, especially those willingly employed in public administration and policy programs, want to be counselors to the powerful, as well as to be basic scientists. Regardless of individual styles, collectively we all want a marriage of modes of inquiry that promises to be both generalizable and useful.

Processes result from history, which is economic, geographic, cultural, and political. A tough task is to measure that history and those processes so as to identify where deeds can make a difference, given the constraints of processes. Further, we want to measure differences in processes (e.g., administrative procedures) to find out how malleable they are so we know if reforms are possible and how consequential they are for variations in policy so we will know if reforms will make any difference.

It will help clarify the argument if we can gain appreciation of the contributions of numerous foci and methods of inquiry to this marriage. They may be considered as five dimensions along which the study and teaching of policy and administration may be arranged, as listed in Table 7.2.

The marriage I noted earlier called for the identification of most probable levers in the policy process while taking account of resources and constraints. Constraints and resources are much more than economic considerations, although those have been a central focus of much policy research. But in reaching beyond economic elements, I do not mean to highlight politics in the sense often used by economists. With some economists politics and administration are customarily the error terms in policy models. Political and administrative variance, however, is more than a residual. The incorporation of measurable, empirically testable endogenous political and administrative elements into policy models is not only a worthy goal, it is essential for credible scholarship or advice to the prince(ss).

If political and administrative variables are not measurable and their contributions are not empirically testable, there is no political *science*. There is only guesswork. And experienced politicians or journalists will outguess the speculative academic every time. Are political concepts such as participation, decentralization, competition, or even some more fuzzy favorites such as power or democracy any less measurable than such economic concepts as utility, marginality, efficiency, benefit, or productivity? The difference is more in the mode of record-keeping than in the scientific status of measurability.

A view from the vantage of comparative policy analysis will help reinforce the point.

The Comparative Policy Model

In the late 1960s, I published an article with a fancy graphic model (see Figure 7.1) to guide comparative policy research (Hofferbert,

Table 7.2 Dimensions Along Which the Labor Is Divided

1. Alternative academic subfields:

    Public management
    Planning
    Public administration
    Comparative politics
    Legislative behavior
    Public law
    Local / regional government
    International relations/
        organizations
    Organizational behavior
    Development economics

2. Alternative entry points
   in the policy process:

    Decision making —
        "ex ante" analyses
    Implementation—
        "process" analyses
    Evaluation —
        "ex post" analyses

3. Substantive foci (examples):

    Environmental policy
    Health policy
    Education policy
    Agricultural policy
    Transportation policy

4. Alternative sites:

    Jurisdictional
        International
        National
        Cantonal/states
        Municipal

    Area / Culture
        Developing
        countries
        Western Europe
        Africa
        Single countries

5) Tools of Analysis:

    Survey research
    Aggregate data
    Time series
    Case studies
    Simulation
    Benefit / cost
    Micro / Macro modeling
    Decision analysis
    Linear programming

1968). Much to my pleasure, it was discovered in the late 1970s and used in imaginative ways (Mazmanian and Sabatier, 1980a).

The dependent variable(s) of the model are policy outputs: regulations, expenditures, and the like. The model seeks to show the complex, multicausality of policy systems. Implicitly, it suggests that the flexibility of policy makers in any finite period may be constrained by a host of largely uncontrollable (at least in the short run) factors.

Viewed from a contemporary perspective, especially after the development of policy evaluation in the 1970s, the model has two major

Figure 7.1   Model for the Comparative Study of Policy Formation

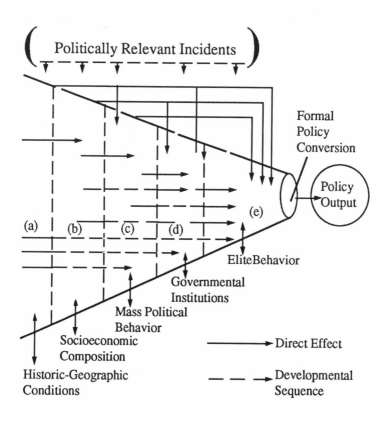

weaknesses. First, it is weak in accounting for feedback over time. It can be made dynamic but not in any obvious manner (see Hofferbert and Schäfer, 1982; see also Chapter 4, Figure 4.3). Thus it says nothing about the systemic, or dynamic, or ongoing impact of policy on society, politics, and so on. That is, it puts the chief emphasis on policy as a dependent variable, whereas proper systems thinking would be much more dynamic. Further, the adviser to the prince(ss) should be most concerned about the consequences of policy and be concerned with the causes of policy only insofar as he or she is able to identify the constraints and resources defining the prince(ss)'s range of choice. The second major weakness is that, since the model deemphasizes policy impact, it is virtually silent on implementation or administration. Therefore, it does not adequately show how research should be conducted on the potential for reform of decision making or reform of implementation and administrative procedures. If these severe limitations are kept in mind, the old model will help focus a discussion of the division of labor in policy analysis.

When first presented, this model was fitted to the context of a literature that reported aggregate data analyses, at the cross-national or at the subnational level. Some additional studies were using time points in single jurisdictions as the unit of analysis.

All early comparative policy studies employed variations on regression analysis to assess the relative contributions of measures of the different sectors of the model to variance in policy outputs. Both the cross-sectional and the longitudinal studies of the 1960s and 1970s were experimenting with diverse measures for historic conditions (usually handled in a narrative manner or as a way to account for residuals), socioeconomic conditions, political control and behavior, and institutional variations (see Hofferbert, 1972, for a review of the literature up to that date).

Most of the data on these sectors of the model were drawn from census sources. Some very interesting scales were constructed for measuring variance in policy. Often, but not always, it was indicated by expenditures for various functions.

Because of the difficulties of measurement and the poverty of appropriate theory, attitudes or behavior of elites (those whose choice should be greatest) were rarely measured directly, but rather equated with the residual once the other elements of the model had been correlated with a particular set of policy indicators (see, however, Mazmanian and Sabatier, 1980a). Theory was and still is light. Induction, guided by previous insights of less technically rigorous scholarship, has driven the inquiry.

The early research stimulated a debate about which is more important, economic or sociocultural constraints, on one hand, or political and governmental institutional variables, on the other. When structured in that manner, political and institutional variables did not fare well, usually coming out as much less relevant than socioeconomic conditions as correlates of policy variance.

Once statistical methods such as path analysis became more common, this either/or mode of discussion subsided, leaving a much more sophisticated picture of the developmental processes between social change, economic resources, political institutions, and policy products (Cnudde and McCrone, 1969; Lewis-Beck, 1977; Hofferbert and Urice, 1985).

This debate led to a body of marvelously cumulative empirical research, which was almost totally ignored by economists, most public administrationists, and nearly all specialists in either specific policy domains or specific foreign areas around the world. Yet it is precisely in the context of this comparative literature that one can begin seeing how socioeconomic structure, politics, and administrative conditions can be measured and empirically analyzed as constraints and resources in a policy system.

One early misdirection was the drive that I and many others conducted to try to extract maximum variance out of the model, with little attention to applications. Of course, if we could show that virtually all of the variance in policy outputs was attributable to socioeconomic, political, and institutional variables, we were, by implication if not by explication, saying that so-called elites have no choice.

That is ''basic research'' at its most elegant level of irrelevance, where it tells the prince(ss) that there is no choice. It is a fine way of chronicling human futility but not much aid to the prince(ss) or the wise counselor. It says that the only way to change policy is to change social, economic, and political structures—a revolution, if you will. This is rarely the advice the prince(ss) wants to hear.

Fortunately for the prince(ss) and the counselors, none of us in comparative policy analysis was ever able to explain more than about half of the variance in anything, leaving a lot of room for choice by the prince(ss). But few members of royal houses were listening anyway.

After some years pursuing a high R^2, I realized that if I were interested in application of policy analysis, in advising the prince(ss), I may not want a high R^2. If one can show, with a well-specified model, that there is a very low amount of policy variance explained by factors leading up to the elite behavior sector of the model, then one may conclude that most of the existing variance is the result of choices by relevant elites (see Mazmanian and Sabatier, 1980a).

Alternatively, if it can be shown that certain institutional or political practices are relevant to policy variance, but are themselves somewhat independent of historical, social, or economic determination (i.e., the paths up to institutions have low coefficients), but if those same institutional or political practices do have a measurable impact on policy, we can conclude that changes (reforms) in those practices are attainable and would have predictable consequences for policy.

Such a finding allows us to say to the prince(ss): "Sorry, Your Highness, today you can't do much to change the policy. But if you look outward a bit, you can reform your political and institutional practices, which, in turn, will—over the longer run—give you the tools to attain the objectives you seek."

Likewise, if we have an empirically reliable research base, we will understand the linkage between policy pronouncements, implementation practices, and social results. When we have that base, we can say to the prince(ss): "Look, Your Highness, if you change administrative procedures X and Y, you can expect policy A to have result Z. Otherwise, forget about policy A."

These conversations take place only after a thorough accounting of the constraints imposed on policy choice and on institutional reform by historical, cultural, and economic forces. If the counselor is up-to-date and smart, that accounting will include use of rather sophisticated comparative analysis. The variance potentially controllable by the prince(ss) through institutional means, after facing those larger constraints, may not be worth the bother. Assessing the worth of bother is something at which princes and princesses are usually very good.

The Division of Labor: Revisited

There is no need to revise the division of labor: not across alternative academic subfields, not across different substantive foci, not between alternative entry points, not for alternative sites, and not for alternative tools of analysis. Many (maybe most) scientific priorities such as those presented in Table 7.2 are defensible.

Disciplinary territoriality and tunnel vision, however, are not defensible. Most academics live inside organizational structures that encourage a narrow range of discursive interaction. The new public administration-policy programs now aborning or undertaking reform have an extraordinary opportunity.

Public administrationists and/or policy analysts may dispute the relative virtues of case analysis versus aggregate comparison. But there are grounds for agreeing on the need to be explicit about what central dimensions of variance in administrative practices are likely to affect variance in policy delivery.

Even if one had a census of administrative practices, it would be difficult to be sure in what priority they should be investigated. For that, we need insightful case studies, of high internal validity. But those who write case studies need to look sympathetically on the task of testing hypotheses, not to condemn it as ivory tower rhetoric but to offer guidance on conceptualization, measurement, and priorities. That requires aggregate data analysts who are willing to listen to stories about administrative practices and problems in places from Swiss communes to Thai bureaucracies. It requires likewise that the case analyst take guidance from comparative work and look carefully for the real objects that are so poorly reflected in aggregate data analyses.

Case studies may be specific as to locale or substantive policy content. One who studies environmental policy in a few small settings may know more about air pollution control than ought to be allowed for a social scientist. Likewise, teams of scholars may collectively know a lot about the specific histories and institutional circumstances of environmental policy making and implementation in several countries.

If case analysts insist, however, that everything is unique, that every case is totally different from every other, not only does it deny the potential for building generalizable knowledge, but it also denies the analyst's own status as an expert. If what has been studied is unique, it is of no use when one confronts a new situation or problem somewhere or sometime else. If the analysis of environmental policy in one country is unique, the analyst has nothing to say to policy makers in another country. I suspect that this is not true. I suspect most case analysts have more transferable knowledge than they care to admit in print.

Further, not only is this knowledge transferable from one locale to another, but I strongly suspect that insight is transferable, in some predictable fraction, to other substantive areas of policy, even so seemingly far removed as health, education, or transportation.

One problem, as noted in Chapter 2, is that specialized policy research is most often published in places not frequented by either policy theorists or persons from other substantive or regional foci. And if one is heavily involved in, for example, environmental policy work, (s)he is unlikely routinely to read the journals that carry material about other policies.

If one were able to build aggregate indicators of the concepts in case studies, again for example, about environmental policy, and use them to test hypotheses on fifty countries extensively rather than on one or a few intensively, perhaps in other substantive policies, the case analyst might gain a better appreciation of potential generalizations in her or his own work.

Case analysts who are sympathetic to that undertaking can, in turn, be more attentive to the usual rather than the unusual in reporting intensive work. Likewise, they can be attuned to the impact of extensive work in the search for intensive explanations.

In beginning to apply comparative policy analysis and evaluation techniques in various Third World settings, for example, one must be alert not only to that which is unique but to that which is common with past research. This is a lesson addressed in Chapter 4. In countries that for understandable cultural reasons have relied heavily on imported analytical tactics, there comes a stage in the evolution of social science when there is political and ideological pressure for "indigenization" (Uchida, 1985). If such efforts are only thinly disguised attempts to roll back the clock on scientific progress, a retreat from rigor into causal pontification, they are hardly laudable. One should endorse appropriate caution about the fit of imported research priorities. But we must also be alert to that which is only superficially unique, lest we lose all capacity for spotting patterns.

The admonition to view contributions of alternative policy analytic foci and priorities in terms of their capacity to sort the determinants of policy outputs and impacts according to their relative degree of controllability seems to me to be an eminently exportable bit of advice.

How might this work in practice for the counselor to the prince(ss), for the adviser who would rather speak truth to the powerful than tell lies to the weak? First, understand the constraints upon and resources available to those who make policy decisions. That is, identify the range of real choice, given social, political, economic, and process limits.

Caution:
Do not accept the prince(ss)'s word. Some rulers overestimate their limits and underestimate their options.
Task:
Compare policies pursued by other principalities with various constraints, resources, and processes (today or in the past). The lower the correlations, the greater the chance that the ruler has room for choice. Wise analogies (i.e., good comparative research) are the counselor's best friends.

Second, minimize the chances of the prince(ss) making stupid policy choices, that is, reduce error between choice of instruments and policy goals.

Caution:
Common sense oversimplifies and is often wrong, and honest effort does not equal good results.
Task:
Compare results of policies at other times and places. Wise analogies (i.e., good comparative research) are the counselor's best friends.

If processes (e.g., decision-making practices) prevent wise choices, consult other experiences to ascertain which reforms would facilitate wiser choice of policy. If processes (e.g., bureaucracy, "implementation") prevent wisely chosen policies from having beneficial results, consult other experience to ascertain which reforms have the most promise. The overall tasks of the analyst-counselor are to measure key concepts for valid analogies; control for alternative causes; and listen sympathetically to what other analysts have to say, even if they use slightly different research strategies or come from other academic playing fields. That is, leave the search for territorial sovereignty to the prince(ss).

8

Policy Evaluation, Political Science, and Democratic Theory

Not every political scientist wants to spend time and energy communing with bureaucrats (see Chapters 1, 2, and 3), studying implementation processes in the Third World (see Chapters 4, 5, and 6), or collaborating with economists and other disciplinary foreigners (see Chapter 7). Many political scientists, who might even agree with the prescriptions of this book, will wish to continue studying politics, as politics has traditionally been defined. That is what the members of the disciplinary craft have done best for several generations. I urge them to stick to their lasts. But bear with me just a bit more.

Why has the profession of political science been so inhospitable to policy evaluation? Why, for example, do the major disciplinary journals not carry more articles reporting empirical assessments of specific public programs? Why do so many books on policy analysis have no citations to the rich cumulative body of empirical research testing the linkage between politics and policy? And what possible connection could there be between policy evaluation and democratic theory, as is implied by the title of this chapter?

Some attention to the professional and career aspects of this unease were addressed in Chapter 2. But there are deeper barriers than career considerations to the full acceptance of policy analysis by the discipline of political science or for the recognition by many policy analysts of the policy relevance of political science.

Policy evaluation, as it has evolved over the past several years, has indeed engaged the energies of many political scientists. But the enterprise of assessing the impact of policy on society still remains notably angular, if not irrelevant, to many of the traditional concerns of political scientists. Since it would be hard to argue that political scientists have (or ought to have) no interest in what governments produce, this angularity is, at first, puzzling.

Policy evaluation takes an unequivocally instrumental view of government. Governments are there to do things to and for the members of a polity. Health policy is to improve people's health. Education policy is to educate people. Transport policy is to transport people and goods from place to place. Policy evaluators even call government outputs "instruments."

The disciplinary array of analysts who evaluate such instruments is wide. Public health specialists evaluate health policy. Education specialists evaluate education policies. Economists are unusually transpolicy, in that they show up in several substantive domains whenever money or a close approximation of money is involved. Many political scientists have joined the business of evaluating policy instruments (see, for example, Nachmias, 1980). Some universities have even dedicated their political science curricula principally to that task (SUNY-Binghamton's graduate programs, for example).

Most political scientists, however, have never been wholly comfortable with a highly instrumental, mechanistic view of political and government activity. Most of us have been exposed to if not immersed in Western political philosophy, from Plato through J. S. Mill to modern democratic theory. Most of us implicitly give high priority to questions derived from one or another version of a democratic model.

The frameworks of discourse in which we have been trained and in which we work tilt our curiosity toward questions of democratic governance and democratic citizenship. Citizenship is never wholly instrumental. Neither are the institutional contexts within which that citizenship is exercised. Democratic citizenship, in particular, is commonly, if implicitly, an element of or an equivalent to the good life, not exclusively a means to a higher-quality life. Citizenship is self-justifying.

Politics and Policy as Intrinsic Rather Than Instrumental

POLITICS AS INTRINSIC

We are admonished in school and in the media to vote. It is our civic duty. We are to vote not to obtain something. Here is a major point of significant noncommunication between political scientists and economists and the reason why economic models have a checkered record in political science inquiry. Economists' models rarely accept politics as intrinsic rather than instrumental. People are to vote or otherwise act out their citizenship as an intrinsically moral act. Likewise, democratically invested legislatures debate and executives speak primarily for the moral nature of the act, not for the ends the act attains. The activity, the discourse, contains within it the end for which it takes place. The Athenian and the modern democrat exist to be citizens. They are not citizens as a means to a further end. Citizenship, through dialogue and positive action, engages the person in the public definition of morality. And that action equals the good life.

Argument about the feasibility of direct democracy, or the outmoded nature of the town meeting, has clouded the issue of democratic citizenship. If the action is the objective, it matters little if the action is efficient or if it takes place within a particular formal setting. Public discourse is as meaningful over a beer in the local saloon or within the family in front of the TV as it is in the Forum.

In some respects, citizenship was more awkward for the Athenian than for the modern postmaterialist member of the democratic masses. Somebody has to till the fields, produce the goods, and otherwise mind the store while people are busy being citizens. Slaves and women put in long days minding the store for the Athenians. They did not have a thirty-seven-hour week. In contrast, a highly productive private economy, set off somewhat from the political arena, ensures the relative autonomy of politics and also provides the material wherewithal for the modern masses to enjoy the equivalent of the precious, aristocratic monopoly of leisure essential to classical citizenship. Constitutional opportunity combined with mass literacy may make ordinary folks today as good at citizenship as were the few privileged Athenians.

Aside from relative assessment of how well democracy functions, that democratic citizenship is itself an end state, an intrinsically moral objective, has conditioned the approaches and uncertainties of modern political science toward policy analysis. Again, if democratic citizenship is the end and not a means, then it is minimally relevant to dispute the effects of democracy on something else, such as policy variance. Formal policy-making institutions exist not merely to make policy but as intrinsic elements of a (democratic) moral collectivity.

Dialogue, as in an elected legislature or between an elected executive and the media, is itself an end. We speak of the quality of public dialogue as a value by its form, irrespective of its content. Thus we judge our elite-mass communication, or our legislatures, or our electoral mechanisms as they fit to an implicit model of how democracy works, not what the structures do or produce.

POLICY AS INTRINSIC

Substantive policy and implementation processes, likewise, have an intrinsic moral element which exists apart from their instrumental value. Can a policy be characterized as manifestation of public will or of the democratic process? Is the policy a firm and clear statement of moral priorities? If so, then it is to be (meta?) politically valued and approved, irrespective of the mechanical linkages between policy instruments and sustained or changed social conditions.

The War on Poverty was "good" because it stated so vigorously our democratic and collective opposition to poverty, whether or not it made a scintilla of difference to the physical or fiscal well-being of anybody. The War on Cancer or the War on Drugs or the "moral equivalent of war" on energy conservation are appropriately evaluated not merely as cures for cancer, prevention of drug abuse, or conservation of energy. Their intrinsic, as opposed to instrumental, worth is the clarity with which they affirm collective moral priorities.

Democracy provides the dynamic element of the moral search. It provides incentives for political leaders to seek points of disagreement on moral priorities and to articulate competitive alternatives. And dialogue is guaranteed continuation by the evolving content and lack of normative unanimity combined with institutional and constitutional guarantees of discourse.

So long as the accoutrements of democratic processes produce moral affirmations that resonate and articulate sympathetically, a democratic system sustains its reason for being and its legitimacy. Public problems do not get "solved." They get affirmed and managed. Seen this way, no policy is ever finished or completed, once enacted, any more than a Christian's connection to God is made permanent by a single utterance of the Apostles' Creed. The Lord's Prayer must be repeated not because God forgets but because morality is made manifest through repeated affirmation. And because the institutions themselves (voting, public dialogue) embody a moral statement of "how people should be governed," their permanence assures the continuity of affirmation, dialogue, and adjustment of moral priorities.

This focus on the noninstrumental or intrinsic aspect of the democratic process and its policy products should not be read as an exercise in cynicism. Rather, it is an effort to direct attention to the essentially normative functions of governance and the normative commitment of the discipline of political science to democratic forms of governance as end rather than as instrument for getting some specific or specifiable state of socioeconomic affairs.

A concern with the intrinsic rather than the instrumental in the governmental process need not serve as an excuse or apology for ineffective policies. Policies that bungle their mechanical objectives, by missing the mark, by negative side effects, or by being too costly, undermine the clarity of their moral statement. Thus the reported "failures" of the War on Poverty and the theory it embodied, as discussed in Chapter 1, had the effect of clouding the statement made by those policies. Likewise, when President Nixon obtained the elimination of the Office of Economic Opportunity (OEO) and the folding into regular departments of the surviving programs of the War on Poverty, the critics were more distressed with the nature of the message than with the diminution of actual programmatic effort. Yet Nixon could make such a move precisely because, by virtue of negative program evaluations, the OEO had lost some of its moral force.

Some policies cannot be evaluated by standards other than their affirmation of moral priority. Such is clearly the case with capital punishment. The deterrent effect of capital punishment or the cost of executing criminals are of modest relevance when weighed against the conflicting norms of social retribution versus the distastefulness of officially taking a human life (Berns, 1979).

In democratic systems, much dialogue and disputation concern the relative vigor with which alternative policies affirm normative commitment. The absence of stronger national gun control laws, regardless of whether such laws would reduce violent crime, strikes some people as a weak moral stance. Moral dialogue even gets quantified, as in disputes over how much is spent rather than what is bought with budgetary allocations. Debate over peace through national defense versus peace through reduced armaments is engaged in the defense budget. How much or how little is spent on alternative public programs becomes itself a metric of moral priority, giving force to the claim that a budget is "political philosophy in numbers."

Moral priorities are neither universal nor stagnant. People differ and change in what they believe to be collectively good. Perhaps the highest form of democratic citizenship is to have a large zone of uncertainty about matters of vital moral importance, to believe with equal passion in a moral condition and in the right of others to criticize that position (Hofferbert, 1986b).

Those who went beyond certain limits of civility in the antiwar movement still justify their actions on the grounds that they were trying to stop wanton killing in Vietnam. Members of the Right-to-Life movement oppose abortion on the grounds that they too are trying to stop killing. The overlap in beliefs of these two sets, to the extent that there is any, is in their mutual commitment (however implicit) to the processes of democratic dialogue. The more zealous they are in saving lives, the lower that commitment. But less important than the commitment of small groups of zealots to democracy is the extent to which otherwise quiet citizens will be aroused by callous disregard for democratic rules. Thus many otherwise left-leaning people were aroused to oppose the violence and other antidemocratic elements of the antiwar movement of the 1960s and 1970s. Otherwise right-leaning citizens oppose the bombing (but perhaps not the picketing) of abortion clinics in the 1980s. For both of these moderating groups, the process is more fundamentally valuable than even the saving of life itself, whether in Vietnam or in the womb.

Political science, in both its philosophic and its social scientific bent, more than other disciplines, is centrally concerned with the processes of citizenship. It is small wonder, then, that moves to substitute the dependent variables of other fields have not been hospitably received by political science. The conceptual elements and measurement tactics, the independent and dependent variables, may often have been common to several disciplines: psychology, economics, anthropology, sociology, and even business management. But the theoretical center of gravity has remained for political scientists uniquely *political* and *governmental*.

It is also small wonder that the two major categories of policy analysis to emerge on the disciplinary scene in recent years, comparative policy output research and evaluation research, have sounded rather dissonant tones. The early mechanistic message of comparative policy output research cast doubt on the relevance of politics, as traditionally conceived, to the products of government action (Dawson and Robinson, 1963; Cutright, 1965; Dye, 1966; Hofferbert, 1966). Policies of governments are prima facie important. Yet if they are immune to citizen participation, election results, or modes of representation, our traditional normative and empirical priorities are in jeopardy. Those democratic theoretic norms say that the instruments by which people choose their policy makers should be effective in conditioning what those policy makers produce. If the party composition of a legislature changes, for example, that change should be reflected in changes in policy.

But early research failed to provide unequivocal support for this simple formula. Fortunately, the elaboration and sophistication of comparative policy output research have long since "reinstated" politics in the policy process (e.g., Jennings, 1979; Mazmanian and Sabatier, 1980a; Flora and Heidenheimer, 1981b; Castles, 1982; Schmidt, 1982).

Policy evaluation, the examination of the social consequences of government actions, has, on the other hand, been too mechanistic and instrumental to be fitted to the traditional, implicit democratic theory model that guides most political scientists. Evidence of this disjunction is readily apparent if one compares contents of journals. Political scientists (i.e., academics with doctorates in political science and employed by political science faculties or departments) regularly publish evaluation research in such journals as the *Policy Studies Review, Politics and Policy,* the *Journal of Public Policy,* the *Policy Studies Journal,* or others further from the discipline. Rarely, however, does one find an example of such work in the *American Political Science Review.* Rarely is policy evaluation research supported by the Political Science Program of the U.S. National Science Foundation.[1]

An argument can be made for such exclusivity. When political scientists act like health researchers or economists, they ought to compete for research support or publication space with health researchers or economists, leaving the precious few resources of political science to those nearer the core of the discipline.

Politics as Dependent Variable

Comparative policy output research deviated from disciplinary tradition by treating political conditions as independent variables, that is, as instruments for determining the shape of policy content. Politics, in that sense, should *do* something, rather than *be* something. I propose a reversal of that equation, that is, to view politics as the dependent variable of policy. How do variations in policy patterns affect citizenship at the micro level or democratic institutions at the macro level? The tactics of evaluation research are amenable to these questions.

Governments are consequential actors in contemporary societies. Public policies make a difference in people's lives, sometimes for the better, sometimes for the worse. Is it not reasonable for us to investigate the consequences of public policies for people's political lives? If the purpose of democratic politics is to legitimize and maximize the breadth of moral discourse, how is that process itself built, sustained, or eroded by the decisions of policy makers?

Do broad historical differences in the products of state actions affect the attributes of individual behaviors which we consider key to democratic citizenship? Do different education systems, different health and welfare systems, or different economic policy patterns alter in measurable ways the different modes of citizens' engagement with the polity?

Likewise, at the macroinstitutional level, we should be able to probe the associations (if not causal linkages) between general patterns of state activity and the ebb and flow of democratization. Policies affect the structure, performance, and viability of economies. May they not also be hypothesized to affect the structure, performance, and viability of polities? Does investment in human services, for example, enhance the commitment of masses to their democratic roles? Or does too much government breed docility and cynicism, eroding civic norms?[2]

Empirical democratic theoretical inquiry would do well to take advantage of the lessons and tactics of policy evaluation. Policy evaluation is not so much a set of analytical techniques as it is a mode of thinking about relationships among elements of the policy process. It highlights concern for complex interrelationships and discourages oversimplification through monocausal explanations.

My proposal is that political scientists, by adopting and adapting policy evaluation tactics, can make significant progress in linking the currently disconnected fields of policy evaluation and democratic theory.[3] Policy evaluation heretofore has tracked the impact of government actions ("instruments") on social conditions. My fundamental proposal is that we add to the focus an effort to track the impact of policy on political conditions as well.

Notes

Chapter 1

The original version of this essay was delivered to the Swiss Society for Public Administration, Bern, Switzerland, 17 November 1985.

1. Much of this chapter reflects the impact of Aaron Wildavsky's *Speaking Truth to Power* (1979), arguably the most attractive collection of aphorisms, most of which are probably true, about our craft currently in print. For an excellent brief analytical review of the rise, with less attention to the apparent decline, of evaluation "institutions," see Haveman, 1987. Haveman also does a very good job of sketching how policy analysis has become institutionalized (and thus less visible) in such federal settings as the General Accounting Office, the Congressional Budget Office, and the Office of Technology Assessment. This process, at the state and local levels, is discussed here in Chapter 2.

2. The classic formulation is in Donald Campbell, "Reforms as Experiments" (1969). An even more detailed exposition, brought up to date in light of twenty years of policy evaluation, is Joseph S. Wholey's *Evaluation and Effective Public Management* (1983).

3. The percentage of persons aged sixty-five and older below the poverty line has, in recent years, been only slightly above the average in poverty for the total population. This represents a drop since 1960, when the elderly poverty rate was twice the total rate. Between 1970 and 1985, median family income rose 2.6 percent, whereas average Social Security payments rose by 49 percent. In the four years between 1980 and 1984, median income of all households increased, in constant dollars, by 5.1 percent. The median income of those over sixty-five increased by 13.7 percent in the same period.

4. See, for a bit of corrective to this pessimistic inventory, John E. Schwarz's *America's Hidden Success: A Reassessment of Twenty Years of Public Policy* (1988).

162

Chapter 2

The original version of this chapter was delivered at the Second Workshop on Development and Present State of Public Policy Research: Country Studies in Comparative Perspective, Science Center–Berlin, December 1984.

1. This prediction and the processes underlying it are clearly elaborated in Renfrow and Gow (1985). They trace the history of public administrative training in the United States and see a more analytical role for the public manager as a logical marriage of current training trends and today's technology.

2. That comparable developments in public service training are taking place outside the United States is illustrated clearly by Susan Richards (1985).

Chapter 3

The original version of this chapter was delivered to the seminar in "L'informatique dan le Administrations et Enterprises Publique," Institut de Hautes Etudes en Administration Publique, Lausanne, Switzerland, 28 October 1985.

1. This finding was apparently rather controversial. My colleagues and I sought several times to get papers published in the major gerontology journals. None would accept them for publication. Maybe we did a poor job of writing. But maybe there were other reasons for rejection. Reviewers recommended against publication on the grounds that the findings were obviously in error, although no technical flaws were noted (leaving the implication that we must be lying). Some said that the findings should not be published because they were dangerous to a valuable program.

Chapter 4

The original version of this essay was presented to the Annual Joint Workshops of the European Consortium for Political Research, Aarhus, Denmark, in April 1982. A modified version was published in the *Journal of Public Policy* 5 (1985): 87–105.

1. For a relevant theoretical elaboration, see Schmidt, 1982.

2. An exception would be evaluations by political scientists of the causes and consequences of macroeconomic policy. See, for example, Cameron, 1978; Hibbs, 1978; Schmidt, 1982. For a diagnosis of the division-of-labor problem presented by policy analysis to political science, see Chapters 7 and 8.

3. Using World Bank definitions of "middle income" to include fifty countries, ranging in GNP per capita from Ghana ($420) to Israel ($4,500) in 1981,

of which most generous definitions of pluralist democracy would not fit more than six or eight (World Bank, 1982). For a fairly intensive examination of Turkey's most recent effort to redemocratize, see Ergüder and Hofferbert, 1983.

Chapter 6

An earlier version of this essay was presented to the Annual Meeting of the Southern Political Science Association, Savannah, Georgia, November 1984.

Chapter 7

The original version of this essay was delivered to the Research Colloquium of the Institut de hautes etudes en administration publique, Lausanne, Switzerland, 30 October 1985.

1. For a related view, which reveals interesting aspects of the founding logic of one of the leading graduate policy schools, see the Appendix to Aaron Wildavsky's *Speaking Truth to Power* (1979).

Chapter 8

Portions of this chapter were published in *Policy Studies Review* (Hofferbert, 1986a).

1. Few members of our craft are more solidly embedded in the political science discipline than Aaron Wildavsky. Yet after several years as dean of a policy analysis school, he felt compelled to announce in print that he had reclassified himself from political scientist to political economist. We should hope and trust that his election to the presidency of the American Political Science Association has induced him to reevaluate his identity. See his *Speaking Truth to Power* (1979).

2. Zehra Arat has coded developing countries by level of democratization, as well as changes up and down the scale, by commonly employed indicators at annual time points between 1948 and 1978. Although she did not incorporate as independent variables "output" indicators, narrowly conceived, she has provided an impressive analysis of the impact on democratization of such conditions as inflation rates, changes in income levels, and distribution of wealth. The

next step would be to incorporate, to the extent possible with longitudinal data, indicators of policy outputs into the models she develops (Arat, 1984).

3. A very preliminary investigation, for example, shows strong potential linkages between government priorities, in less developed countries, for human services and the sustenance of liberal democratic practices a decade or so later (Hofferbert, 1988).

References

Adelman, Irma, and Cynthia Taft Morris. 1984. "Economic Development and the Distribution of Income." In Seligson, ed., 151–55.

Ahmad, Feroz. 1981. "The Political Economy of Kemalism." In Kazancigil and Özbudun, eds.

Alber, Jens. 1981. "Government Responses to the Challenge of Unemployment: The Development of Unemployment Insurance in Western Europe." In Flora and Heidenheimer, eds., 1981a, 151–86.

Alberti, Giorgio. 1981. *Basic Needs in the Context of Social Change: The Case of Peru*. Paris: OECD.

Arat, Zehra F. 1984. "The Viability of Democracy in Developing Countries." Ph.D. dissertation, State University of New York at Binghamton.

Atar, Serdaz. 1984. "The Distribution of Health Services in a Developing Country: The Case of Turkey." Paper presented at the Annual Meeting of the Southern Political Science Association, Savannah, Ga., November.

Banks, Arthur S. 1984. *Cross-Polity Time Series Data*. Center for Social Analysis, State University of New York–Binghamton.

Barnes, Samuel, Max Kaase, et al. 1979. *Political Action: Mass Participation in Five Western Democracies*. Beverly Hills: Sage.

Berns, Walter. 1979. *For Capital Punishment: Crime and the Morality of the Death Penalty*. New York: Basic Books.

Blaikie, M. Piers, John Cameron, and J. David Seddon. 1981. *The Struggle for Basic Needs in Nepal*. Paris: OECD.

Boratav, Kemal. 1981. "Kemalist Economic Policies and Etatism." In Kazancigil and Özbudun, eds.

Cameron, David R. 1978. "The Expansion of the Political Economy." *American Political Science Review* 72:1243–61.

Campbell, Donald. 1969. "Reforms as Experiments." *American Psychologist* 24:409–29.

Castles, Francis, ed. 1982a. *Do Parties Matter? Politics and Policies in Democratic Capitalist States*. Beverly Hills: Sage.

————. 1982b. "Politics, Public Expenditures and Welfare." In Castles, ed., 1982a, 21–96.

————. 1983. "Academic Autonomy and Policy Relevance: The Case of the British Social Science Research Council." Paper presented at the IPSA Study Group on Public Policy Analysis Workshop on the University/Government Interface, Boğaziçi University, Istanbul, Turkey, August.

Cingranelli, David L., Richard I. Hofferbert, Linda Huff-Redman, and Thomas E. Pasquarello. 1981. *The National Nutrition Program for the Elderly.* Binghamton, N. Y.: Center for Social Analysis.

Cnudde, Charles, and Donald McCrone. 1969. "Party Competition and Welfare Policies in the American States." *American Political Science Review* 63:858–66.

Cutright, Phillips. 1963. "National Political Development: Measurement and Analysis." *American Sociological Review* 28:253–64.

————. 1965. "Political Structure, Economic Development, and National Social Security Programs." *American Journal of Sociology* 30:537–50.

Dawson, Richard, and James Robinson. 1963. "Inter-party Competition, Economic Variables, and Welfare Policies in the American States." *Journal of Politics* 25:265–89.

Downs, Anthony. 1974. "The Successes and Failures of Federal Housing Policy." *Public Interest* 34:124–45.

Dye, Thomas R. 1966. *Politics, Economics and the Public.* Chicago: Rand McNally.

————. 1984. *Understanding Public Policy.* 5th ed. Englewood Cliffs: Prentice-Hall.

Ergüder, Üstün. 1980a. "Internal Migration, Politics and Integration: Turkey." In Rivlin and Helmer, eds., *The Changing Middle Eastern City.* Binghamton, N.Y.: Center for Social Analysis and Program in Southwest Asian and North African Studies.

————. 1980b. "Politics of Agricultural Price Policy in Turkey." In Özbudun and Ulasan, eds., *The Political Economy of Income Distribution in Turkey.* New York: Holmes and Meier.

Ergüder, Üstün, and Richard I. Hofferbert. 1984. "Restoration of Democracy in Turkey? Political Reforms and the Election of 1983." Paper presented at the Eighteenth Annual Meeting of the Middle East Studies Association, San Francisco, November.

Evans, Peter. 1979. *Dependent Development.* Princeton: Princeton University Press.

Flora, Peter, and Jens Alber. 1981. "Modernization, Democratization, and the Development of Welfare States in Western Europe." In Flora and Heidenheimer, eds., 1981a, 37–80.

Flora, Peter, and Arnold J. Heidenheimer, eds. 1981a. *The Development of the Welfare State in Europe and North America*. New Brunswick, N. J.: Transaction Books.

————. 1981b. "Historical Core and Changing Boundaries of the Welfare State." In Flora and Heidenheimer, eds., 1981a, 17–36.

Frank, Andre Gunder. 1978. *Dependent Accumulation and Underdevelopment*. London: Macmillan.

Freeman, Howard E., Peter H. Rossi, and Sonia R. Wright. 1979. *Evaluating Social Projects in Developing Countries*. Paris: OECD.

Frieburghaus, Dieter, and Willi Zimmermann. 1985. *Wie Wird Forschung Relevant?* Bern: Schweizerischer Nationalfonds.

Goulet, Dennis. 1977. *The Cruel Choice: A New Concept in the Theory of Development*. New York: Atheneum.

Gran, Guy. 1983. *Development by People*. New York: Praeger.

Grant, James P. 1978. *Disparity Reduction Rates in Social Indicators*. New York: Overseas Development Council.

Grumm, John. 1973. *A Paradigm for the Study of Legislative Systems*. Beverly Hills: Sage.

Hancock, Donald M. 1982. "Comparing Public Policy: An Assessment." Paper presented at the Annual Meeting of the American Political Science Association, Denver, September.

Haveman, Robert T. 1987. "Policy Analysis and Evaluation Research after Twenty Years." *Policy Studies Journal* 16:191–218.

Hedlund, Ronald, and Chana Nachmias. 1980. "The Impact of CETA on Work Orientations." In Nachmias, ed., 80–114.

Heidenheimer, Arnold, Hugh Heclo, and Carolyn Teich Adams. 1983. *Comparative Public Policy: The Politics of Social Choice in Europe and America*. 2d ed. New York: St. Martin's Press.

Heper, Martin, Chong Lim Kim, and Seong-Tong Pai. 1980. "The Role of Bureaucracy and Regime Types." *Administration and Society* 12:137–57.

Hibbs, Douglas. 1978. "Political Parties and Macroeconomic Policy." *American Political Science Review* 73:44–50.

Hofferbert, Mark R. 1985. "Measuring the Impact of Drinking Water and Sanitation Programs in Rural Nepal." Manuscript, UNICEF-Nepal, Kathmandu.

Hofferbert, Richard I. 1966. "The Relation between Public Policy and Some Structural and Environmental Variables in the American States." *American Political Science Review* 60:73–82.

————. 1968. "Elite Influence in State Policy Formation: A Model for Comparative Inquiry." *Polity* 2:316–44.

————. 1972. "State and Community Output Studies: A Review of Comparative Input-Output Analyses." In J. Robinson, ed., *Political Science Annual, III*. Indianapolis: Bobbs-Merrill.

———. 1974. *The Study of Public Policy*. Indianapolis: Bobbs-Merrill.

———. 1981. "Communication." *American Political Science Review* 75:722–24.

———. 1982. "Differential Program Impact as a Function of Target Need— Or Why Some Good Policies Often Seem to Fail." *Policy Studies Review* 2:279–92.

———. 1985. "Policy Analysis Priorities in the Third World: Basic Needs and the Barefoot Evaluator." Paper presented at the Annual Meeting of the Midwest Political Science Association, Chicago, April.

———. 1986a. "Policy Evaluation, Democratic Theory, and the Division of Scholarly Labor." *Policy Studies Review* 5:511–28.

———. 1986b. "Policy Analysis and Political Morality: A Rejoinder to Anne E. Schneider's Critique of My Prescription for a Scholarly Division of Labor." *Policy Studies Review* 6:233–35.

———. 1988. "The Impact of Policy Choice on Democratic Development in Poorer Countries." Paper presented at the Fourteenth World Congress of the International Political Science Association, Washington, D.C., August.

Hofferbert, Richard I., and David L. Cingranelli. 1980. "Premature Goal Specification and Quantification." In Richard Dunn, ed., *Optimizing Public Policy*. Lexington, Mass.: Lexington Books, 95–108.

Hofferbert, Richard I., and Üstün Ergüder. 1982. "Policy Analysis and Political Science: The Turkish Experience." Paper presented at the Twelfth World Congress of the International Political Science Association, Rio de Janeiro, August.

Hofferbert, Richard I., and Terje Sande. 1976. "The Malleability of the Policy Process: Strategies for More Useful Comparative Analysis." Paper presented at the Annual Joint Workshops, European Consortium for Political Research, Louvain la Neuve, Belgium, April.

Hofferbert, Richard I., and G. Schäfer. 1982. "The Application of General Systems Methodology to the Comparative Study of Public Policy." *International Journal of General Systems* 8.

Hofferbert, Richard, and John Urice. 1985. "Small-Scale Policy: The Federal Stimulus versus Competing Explanations for State Funding of the Arts." *American Journal of Political Science* 29:308–29.

Hope, Kempe R. 1984. *The Dynamics of Development and Development Administration*. Westport, Conn.: Greenwood Press.

Inalçik, Halil. 1964. "The Nature of Traditional Society: Turkey." In R. Ward and D. Rustow, eds., *Political Modernization in Japan and Turkey*, 42–63. Princeton: Princeton University Press.

Inglehart, Ronald. 1977. *The Silent Revolution: Changing Values and Political Styles among Western Publics*. Princeton: Princeton University Press.

————. 1989. *Cultural Shift in Advanced Industrial Societies*. Princeton: Princeton University Press.

Ingraham, Patricia W. and Richard I. Hofferbert. 1981. *Broome County's Elderly: A Needs Assessment Survey for the Office for the Aging*. Binghamton, N. Y.: Center for Social Analysis.

Jennings, Edward T., Jr. 1979. "Competition, Constituencies, and Welfare Policies in American States." *American Political Science Review* 73:414–29.

Johnson, Paul. 1983. *Modern Times: The World from the Twenties to the Eighties*. New York: Harper & Row.

Katz, Daniel, Barbara A. Gutek, Robert Kahn, and Eugenia Burton. 1975. *Bureaucratic Encounters*. Ann Arbor: Institute for Social Research.

Kazancigil, Ali, and Ergun Özbudun, eds. 1981. *Ataturk: Founder of a Modern State*. London: C. Hurst & Co., Ltd.

Kuhnle, Stein. 1981. "The Growth of Social Insurance Programs in Scandinavia: Outside Influences and Internal Forces." In Flora and Heidenheimer, eds., 1981a, 125–50.

Kuznets, Simon. 1953. *Economic Change*. New York: Norton.

Leipziger, Danny M., ed. 1981. *Basic Needs and Development*. Cambridge: Oelgeschlager, Gunn and Hain.

Lewis-Beck, Michael. 1977. "The Relative Importance of Socioeconomic and Political Variables for Public Policy." *American Political Science Review* 71:559–66.

Linz, Juan, ed. 1978. *The Breakdown of Democratic Regimes: Crisis, Breakdown, and Re-equilibration*. Baltimore: Johns Hopkins University Press.

Lipset, Seymour Martin. 1959. "Some Social Requisites of Democracy: Economic Development and Political Legitimacy." *American Political Science Review* 53:69–105.

Mann, Charles K. 1980. "The Effects of Government Policy of Income Distribution: A Case Study of Wheat Production in Turkey since World War II." In Ergun Özbudun and Aydin Ulasan, eds., *The Political Economy of Income Distribution in Turkey*, 197–246. New York: Holmes & Meier.

Mardin, Serif. 1969. "Power, Civil Society, and Culture in the Ottoman Empire." *Comparative Studies in Society and History* 11:258–81.

————. 1971. "Ideology and Religion in the Turkish Revolution." *International Journal of Middle East Studies* 2:197–211.

————. 1973. "Center-Periphery Relations: A Key to Turkish Politics." *Daedulus* 102:169–90.

Mayntz, Renate, and Fritz Scharpf. 1975. *Policy-Making in the German Federal Bureaucracy*. Amsterdam: Elsevier.

Mazmanian, Daniel, and Paul Sabatier. 1980a. "A Multi-Variate Model of Public Policy-Making." *American Journal of Political Science* 24:439–68.

———. eds. 1980b. *Symposium on Successful Policy Implementation, Policy Studies Journal,* Special Issue No. 2, 8.

McCrone, Donald, and Richard Hardy. 1978. "Civil Rights Policies and the Achievement of Racial Economic Equality, 1948–1975." *American Journal of Political Science* 22:1–17.

McGreevey, William Paul, ed. 1981. *Third World Poverty.* Lexington, Mass.: Lexington Books.

Moris, Jon. 1981. *Managing Induced Rural Development.* Bloomington, Ind.: International Development Institute.

Morris, Morris David. 1979. *Measuring the Condition of the World's Poor.* New York: Pergamon Press.

Murdock, William W. 1980. *The Poverty of Nations.* Baltimore: Johns Hopkins University Press.

Nachmias, David, ed. 1980. *The Practice of Policy Evaluation.* New York: St. Martin's Press.

O'Donnell, Guillermo. 1973. *Modernization and Bureaucratic Authoritarianism.* Berkeley: University of California Institute of International Studies.

Palumbo, Dennis, and Elaine Sharp. 1980. "Process versus Impact Evaluation of Community Corrections." In Nachmias, ed., 288–303.

Paul, Samuel. 1982. *Managing Development Programs: The Lessons of Success.* Boulder, Colo.: Westview Press.

Peters, B. Guy. 1978. *The Politics of Bureaucracy: A Comparative Perspective.* New York: Longman.

Pressman, Jeffrey, and Aaron Wildavsky. 1979. *Implementation.* 2d ed. Berkeley and Los Angeles: University of California Press.

Rees, Albert. 1974. "An Overview of the Labor-Supply Results." *Journal of Human Resources* 9:41–63.

Renfrow, Patty, and David John Gow. 1985. "Training Policy Analysts: Past, Present, and Future." Paper presented at the joint workshop on Policy Analysis and Training of Public Servants, Study Group on Public Policy Analysis, IPSA, and the European Institute of Public Administration, Maastrict, Netherlands, July.

Richards, Susan. 1985. "Training for Public Management." Paper presented at the joint workshop on Policy Analysis and Training of Public Servants, Study Group on Public Policy Analysis, IPSA, and the European Institute of Public Administration, Maastricht, Netherlands, July.

Riggs, Fred. 1966. *Thailand.* Honolulu: East-West Center Press.

Rostow, W. W. 1961. *The Stages of Economic Growth: A Non-Communist Manifesto.* New York: Cambridge University Press.

Rustow, Dankwart. 1968. "Ataturk as a Founder of a State." *Daedulus* 97:793–828.

Sabatier, Paul, and Daniel Mazmanian. 1980. "The Implementation of Public Policy: A Framework of Analysis." *Policy Studies Journal,* Special Issue No. 2, 8:538–60.

Schmidt, Manfred. 1982. "The Role of the Parties in Shaping Macroeconomic Policy." In Castles, 1982a, 97–176.

Schumacher, Ernst F. 1973. *Small Is Beautiful: Economics as If People Mattered.* New York: Harper & Row.

Schwarz, John E. 1988. *America's Hidden Success: A Reassessment of Twenty Years of Public Policy.* Rev. ed. New York: Norton.

Scott, James C. 1977. *The Moral Economy of the Peasant.* New Haven: Yale University Press.

Seligson, Mitchell, ed. 1984. *The Gap between Rich and Poor.* Boulder, Colo.: Westview Press.

Sharkansky, Ira. 1978. *Public Administration: Policy-Making in Government Agencies.* 4th ed. Chicago: Rand McNally.

Sharkansky, Ira, and Richard I. Hofferbert. 1969. "Dimensions of State Politics, Economics, and Public Policy." *American Political Science Review* 63.

Stokey, E., and R. Zeckhauser. 1978. *A Primer for Policy Analysis.* New York: Norton.

Streeten, Paul. 1979. "Basic Needs: Premises and Promises." *Journal of Policy Modelling,* 136–46 (World Bank Reprint Series, No. 62).

Sunar, Ilkay. 1974. *State and Society in the Politics of Turkey's Development.* Ankara: Faculty of Political Science, Ankara University.

———. 1981. "Consolidation of Democracy as a Problem and Prospect in Turkey: An Agenda for Research." Paper presented at the Berliner Institute für Vergleichende Sozialforschung, December.

Todaro, Michael. 1981. *Economic Development in the Third World.* 2d ed. New York: Longman.

Uchida, Takeo. 1985. "Issues and Perspectives in Political Science in Asia and the Pacific." *Participation* 9:9–23.

Verba, Sidney, Norman Nie, and Jong-Lim Kim. 1978. *Participation and Political Equality: A Seven-Nation Comparison.* Cambridge: Cambridge University Press.

Von Beyme, Klaus. 1985. "Plea for Policy Analysis." *Participation* 9:30–33.

Walker, Jack. 1969. "The Diffusion of Innovations among the American States." *American Political Science Review* 63:880–89.

Weede, Erich. 1985. *Entwicklungsländer in der Weltgesellschaft*. Wiesbaden: Westdeutscher Verlag.

Weiss, Charles, and Nicolas Jequier, eds. 1984. *Technology, Finance, and Development: An Analysis of the World Bank as a Technological Institution*. Lexington, Mass.: Lexington Books.

Wholey, Joseph S. 1983. *Evaluation and Effective Public Management*. Boston: Little, Brown.

Wildavsky, Aaron. 1979. *Speaking Truth to Power: The Art and Craft of Policy Analysis*. Boston: Little, Brown.

Wilensky, Harold. 1975. *The Welfare State and Equality*. Berkeley and Los Angeles: University of California Press.

Wollmann, Helmut. 1983. "The State of the Art in the Federal Republic of Germany." Paper presented at the IPSA Study Group on Public Policy Analysis Workshop on the University/Government Interface, Boğaziçi University, Istanbul, Turkey, August.

Wollmann, Helmut, Georg Thurn, and Peter Wagner. 1985. "Introducing Policy Research in Developing Countries: Are There Lessons to Be Learned from Developed Countries, Such as Italy and Spain?" Paper presented at the Thirteenth World Congress of the International Political Science Association, Paris, July.

World Bank. 1982. *World Development Report: 1981*. New York: Oxford University Press.

———. 1984. *World Development Report: 1984*. New York: Oxford University Press.

———. 1988. *World Development Report: 1988*. New York: Oxford University Press.

Yumer, R. 1980. "Influence du status socio-economique sur la morbidité palundeene: Un essai de mesure." Ph.D. dissertation, Université des Science Sociale de Grenoble.

Index

About the Institute

The University of Alabama established the Institute for Social Science Research in 1984 to promote and conduct social science research. The Institute seeks to advance the theory and methodology of social science disciplines and to respond to society's needs by applying social science to the study of social problems. ISSR is composed of three units: the Center for Social and Policy Analysis, the Capstone Poll, and the Research and Consulting Laboratory. Correspondence should be addressed to:

Institute for Social Science Research
319 ten Hoor Hall
The University of Alabama
Box 870216
Tuscaloosa, Alabama 35487-0216

About the Social Science Monograph Series

The Institute for Social Science Research and The University of Alabama Press publish the Social Science Monograph Series through a cooperative agreement. The Series includes analyses of social problems and theoretical or methodological works that significantly advance social science research in the judgment of Institute social scientists and of two or more anonymous referees. Conclusions expressed in the monographs are those of the authors and do not necessarily reflect the views of ISSR, The University of Alabama, or organizations that provide funds to support Institute research.